MANXMEN
AT SEA IN THE AGE OF NELSON
1760–1815

MANXMEN
AT SEA IN THE AGE OF NELSON
1760–1815

Matthew Richardson

First published in Great Britain in 2024 by
PEN AND SWORD MARITIME
an imprint of
Pen and Sword Books Ltd
Yorkshire – Philadelphia

Copyright © Matthew Richardson, 2024

ISBN 978 1 39904 449 3

The right of Matthew Richardson to be identified as the author of this work has been asserted by him in accordance with the Copyright, Designs and Patents Act 1988.

A CIP record for this book is available from the British Library
All rights reserved. No part of this book may be reproduced or transmitted in any form or by any means, electronic or mechanical including photocopying, recording or by any information storage and retrieval system, without permission from the Publisher in writing.

Typeset in Times New Roman 12/16 by
SJmagic DESIGN SERVICES, India.
Printed and bound in the UK by CPI Group (UK) Ltd.

Pen & Sword Books Ltd incorporates the imprints of Pen & Sword After the Battle, Archaeology, Atlas, Aviation, Battleground, Discovery, Family History, History, Maritime, Military, Naval, Politics, Railways, Select, Social History, Transport, True Crime, Air World, Claymore Press, Frontline Books, Leo Cooper, Praetorian Press, Remember When, Seaforth Publishing and Wharncliffe.

For a complete list of Pen & Sword titles please contact
PEN & SWORD BOOKS LIMITED
George House, Units 12 & 13, Beevor Street, Off Pontefract Road, Barnsley, South Yorkshire, S71 1HN, England
E-mail: enquiries@pen-and-sword.co.uk
Website: www.pen-and-sword.co.uk

or
PEN AND SWORD BOOKS
1950 Lawrence Rd, Havertown, PA 19083, USA
E-mail: uspen-and-sword@casematepublishers.com
Website: www.penandswordbooks.com

Contents

Acknowledgements vi

Introduction viii

Chapter 1   The Seven Years' War 1

Chapter 2   The American War 28

Chapter 3   The Pacific and the Far East 61

Chapter 4   The French Revolutionary Wars 79

Chapter 5   The Napoleonic Wars 113

Epilogue 151

Notes 155

Bibliography 160

Index 162

Acknowledgements

With any project such as this, the list of those who have assisted the author will be a long one. During three years of research for this book, I was aided by many people who gave willingly of their time and expertise, and in no particular order I acknowledge my appreciation of their help below.

Kevin Asplin assisted with research at the National Archives at Kew, and I benefited tremendously from his knowledge of naval records. Dan Walker was generous in allowing me to use extracts from the letters of his ancestor, Major Paul Crebbin. Nigel Crow as always was generous with his advice and knowledge. Frank Cowin kindly allowed me access to his many years of research into the naval history of the Isle of Man, and it is no exaggeration to say that several sections of this book are founded upon Frank's scholarship. I thank him warmly for his generosity in sharing it with me.

Andrew Lambert, Professor of Naval History at King's College, London, offered invaluable advice and help. Members of the Quilliam Group deserve credit for their efforts to ensure that Captain John Quilliam is not forgotten in his native isle, and I express my thanks to them also for their inspiration. Adrian Cain and Christopher Lewin assisted with Manx language aspects of the book, whilst John Robson, a New Zealand-based member of the Captain Cook Society helped me with enquiries. The staff of the State Library of New South Wales were a great help in locating and supplying material relating to William Bligh. The staff of the Manx Museum library (in particular Wendy Thirkettle) were most helpful in allowing me to examine manuscript material.

ACKNOWLEDGEMENTS

Frances Coakley deserves special mention for the *tour de force* which is the *Manx Notebook* website. The sheer quantity of material transcribed thereon makes this site an invaluable resource for researchers, and my work on this project was greatly assisted by my numerous visits to it. Frances Wilkins, who has done much work on this era, commands respect. Dr Josh Smith of the US Merchant Marine Academy, King's Point, New York provided helpful advice, as did Katherine Weston at the Caird Library, Royal Museums Greenwich. It only remains for me to add that any errors of fact or interpretation are of course my own.

Matthew Richardson
Douglas, 2022

Introduction

The book which you are about to read explores the experiences of Manx seafarers in the Georgian era, as fishermen, as captains of merchant ships, as slave traders and in the Royal Navy. In this era the Manx were highly regarded for their skills as seamen, often honed since boyhood, and consequently they were to be found in some of the most dramatic events and bloodiest battles of the age.

Thanks to church schools, the Isle of Man was unusual in the late eighteenth century in having a high standard of literacy among its working and poorer people. This has left us with a rich bounty of first hand, eyewitness testimony from those who went to sea in those years.

This legacy has enabled their stories to be told either in their own words, or in the words of those who were there alongside them; to preserve the authenticity of their ways of speech, their testimony has been edited as little as possible, and original modes of spelling and grammar retained. This brings with it a sense of immediacy, which belies the more than 200 years which separate our world from theirs. Whilst the attitudes and opinions expressed herein may not always be in accord with our values today, they none the less reflect the realities of life at that time.

Chapter 1

The Seven Years' War

Our story begins in the heart of the eighteenth century, in the 1750s. The bulk of the people of the Isle of Man at this time made their living from the sea, either as fishermen around the Manx coast, or as crewmen on vessels trading with Africa, the Americas and elsewhere. The Island was then under the rule of the Dukes of Atholl, and lay outwith the authority of the British government – a situation which was becoming a cause of increasing friction between the two parties. The day-to-day administration was under the control of a Governor, at the time this was Basil Cochrane, whose main duty was to supervise the collection of the Duke's revenues, particularly those derived from the import of goods. The outstanding aspect of Manx commercial life at that time was smuggling, or the 'running trade' as it was known. In most cases, the contraband was brought into the Isle of Man quite openly, the importers paying the comparatively light Manx duties, and the illegality began only when the produce of the Mediterranean, the West Indies and America was run across to England and Scotland.

The Seven Years' War disrupted commerce to a large extent, but after only a couple of years of peace, the world of the Manx mercantile class was again turned upside down, this time by a more direct and permanent attack on their interests – the Revesting Act of 1765 – which brought the Island's customs duties under the control of the British Crown, and with it an end to what had been the main source of income for the Manx of all classes for several generations.

In the 1750s the Duke of Atholl's jurisdiction in the waters of the Irish Sea extended some nine miles out from the shores of the Isle of Man.

far enough, says the historian George Waldron, who was a commissioner appointed by the British Government to observe events in the Island, that it offered easy sanctuary to a merchant ship intent upon evading a revenue cutter. One result of this trade was the growing importance of Douglas in this era. It was the main import and export centre of the Island, with numerous cellars and warehouses in which merchants could store their goods.

There was much tension between the local officials – officers of the Duke – and the customs officers patrolling the nearby coasts, attempting to keep Manx contraband out, and as the decade progressed there was increasing harassment of Manx commerce by the representatives of the British authorities. Captain George Dowe, of the sloop *Sincerity*, belonging to the custom house at Whitehaven, was one such representative. On 26 June 1750, the crew of the *Sincerity* boarded a wherry on which a Manxman named Hugh Read was a hand. Armed with firearms and cutlasses, they said they would cut the wherry's crew to pieces. They brought the wherry alongside the sloop, and Captain Dowe, coming out of the cabin, ordered the crew of the smaller boat to come aboard. One of them, Patrick Cregan, was slower than the rest and the captain struck him with his sword. He said he would not be satisfied until he ran it through their hearts' blood. After they had been kept aboard for three hours and had been threatened with irons, they were allowed to go.

It was said that Captain Dowe intended to do some meritorious thing by force in the Isle of Man, to gain a reputation with the British authorities. After a while some of the smugglers saw no reason why they should pay the Manx duties either, and the result was that goods which had not been 'entered' were constantly being seized, in the name of the Lord of the Isle, by the local revenue officers, styled 'Searchers'. Sometimes these Searchers were resisted, and it was not unknown for riots to break out at Manx ports as a result.

The other main articles of Manx commerce at this time were Guinea goods. These were trade items bought in from the East Indies, which were exported to West Africa to be bartered on the coast for slaves. The Island acted as a clearing house for beads, fabrics and suchlike and many ships called at Douglas to collect these goods. Direct Manx involvement in the so-called 'triangular trade' between Europe, West Africa, the West Indies and back to Europe was also significant, with some fifty-three of the slave ship captains operating out of Liverpool at this time identified as being Manx. In addition, huge numbers of Manx seafarers were employed as crewmen on slave ships out of that port.

The Isle of Man is perhaps unique in that a considerable number of wills made by ordinary people have survived from this era, and we can ascertain from these documents not just the sheer numbers who describe themselves as a 'mariner', but also the fact that a voyage off the coast of Africa or to the West Indies was undertaken with great apprehension, for many of these men knew they would not return. Malaria and other tropical diseases took their toll, and one Manx sailor named William Cottiman wrote from Liverpool to advise that his cousin had died in this way whilst a crewman on a slave ship:

> This with my love to you acquinting [sic] you of my safe arrival here 26 of last month and saw my Brother in Jamaca [sic] he will be aft home in 6 weeks time or thereabout … Remember my love to Bridget Cottiman, and tell her that her son Dan Cottiman cooper is dead butt [sic] the ship will not be at home this 4 or 5 months yet. She may write to Daniel Corlot taylor or Philip Cottiman and they will tell her what she must do to get his effects.

Subsequently his brother wrote to the dead man's mother:

> I received your letter which you said you was informed of your sons Death there is news from the ship and says that there [sic] Cooper is Dead which I am very sorry to hear but we can Do nothing concerning his affairs not till the ship comes home she is att [sic] Barbadoes [sic] now and as soon as she comes home

I shall let you know of it and then you may do as you think proper to come over or no the Ship is called the *Salisbury* the Captains name is Thomas Mastone, and as soon as she comes I shall let you know.[1]

Two other Manx sailors, John and Thomas Bridson, died around the same time aboard the *Duke of Argyle*, another Liverpool slave ship, under the command of Captain John Newton. Newton is particularly remembered for the fact that he underwent a religious conversion, and later when a Church of England minister became a staunch opponent of the Africa Trade. One of his later anti-slavery publications lists, as a reason for abolition, the physical dangers to which slave crews were exposed:

> The loss [of seamen] in the African trade is truly alarming. I admit that many of them are cut off in their first voyage, and consequently, before they can properly rank as seamen; though they would have been seamen if they had lived. But the neighbourhood of our sea-ports is continually drained of men and boys to supply the places of those who die abroad; and if they are not all seamen, they are all our brethren and countrymen, subjects of the British government. The people who remain on ship-board, upon the open coast, if not accustomed to the climate, are liable to the attack of an inflammatory fever, which is not often fatal unless the occurrence of unfavourable circumstances makes it so ... Strong liquors, such as brandy, rum, or English spirits, the sailors cannot often procure, in such quantities as to hurt them; but they will if they can; and opportunities sometimes offer, especially to those who are in the boats: for strong liquor being an article much in demand, so that without it scarcely a single slave can be purchased, it is always at hand ... The risk of insurrections is to be added. These, I believe, are always

meditated; for the men slaves are not easily reconciled to their confinement and treatment; and, if attempted, they are seldom suppressed without considerable loss; and sometimes they succeed, to the destruction of a whole ship's company at once. Seldom a year passes, but we hear of one or more such catastrophes; and we likewise hear, sometimes, of Whites and Blacks, involved, in one moment, in one common ruin, by the gunpowder taking fire, and blowing up the ship.

As well as these dangers, Newton spoke of the moral corruption to which the crews were subject, as their hearts grew hardened to the savage punishments which they inflicted upon the male slaves, to the advantage which was routinely taken of the female slaves, and to the wanton cruelty of the business generally:

> These instances are specimens of the spirit produced, by the African trade, in men, who, once, were no more destitute of the milk of human kindness than ourselves ... From the women, there is no danger of insurrection, and they are carefully kept from the men; I mean, from the black men ... the captain of an African ship, while upon the coast, is absolute in his command; and if he be humane, vigilant, and determined, he has it in his power to protect the miserable: for scarcely any thing can be done, on board the ship, without his permission, or connivance. But this power is too seldom exerted in favour of the poor women slaves.[2]

Into this already dangerous world of smuggling and slavery was shortly to come another factor. The Seven Years' War had begun incrementally, in 1754, with fighting in the Ohio Territory of North America between forces belonging to the rival colonies of France and Great Britain; it subsequently grew to include other dominions around the world, including British and French possessions in India. At its peak, the war also spread to mainland Europe, with the major protagonists being Great Britain and Prussia on the one hand, and France, Spain and Austria on the other. Although it began far away, the effects of the war were felt locally almost at once. The seas around the Island soon swarmed with privateers, armed merchant ships both British and French, manned by desperate men seeking plunder, in many cases only to be distinguished from pirates by the so called 'letters of marque' which they carried from their respective governments. These documents protected a merchant captain, should he be captured by an enemy power, by proving that he acted under the authority of his government. For many in the Isle of Man the major concern in this conflict would be its disruptive effect upon trade. This was two-fold, for whilst the privateers interfered with the business of the Douglas merchants to a considerable degree by harassing ocean-going vessels in home waters, the naval authorities were also engaged in a ruthless campaign to find seamen for the fleet. Cochrane again wrote to the Duke in May 1755 complaining that:

> When this letter will go from the Island I know not. Boats very seldom goes or comes from the other side, the sailors being affeared of being Pressed by the Men of War who are constantly upon our Coast.[3]

The outbreak of the Seven Years' War had found the Royal Navy woefully undermanned, and as hostilities continued it was increasingly bedevilled by desertion, particularly from its ships when in North American ports. The result was the regular impressment of civilian sailors in Manx waters, in order to make up the shortfall.

> On our coast there is such a warm Press for seamen and lookout for smuglers [sic] that our sales are greatly affected…[4]

So wrote merchant George Moore in 1757 to a French contact with whom he corresponded regularly, regardless of the existing state of war.

THE SEVEN YEARS' WAR

The impressment of Manx seamen from merchant vessels was to be a recurring phenomenon in time of conflict over the next fifty years, and it was via this route that many local seafarers became involved in the Seven Years' War. William Curphy was one such, who was taken from a merchantman and soon found himself in a pitched battle off the shores of West Africa. The enemy-held island fortress of Gorée lay off Dakar on the coast of modern Senegal. Its position gave the French a base from which to menace the British trade route to India, and it was therefore strategically important for Britain to capture it every time she was at war with France. On this occasion, the task was entrusted to Commodore the Honourable Augustus Keppel, who had been sent out after Commodore Marsh's failure against Gorée in May 1758. Ranged against Keppel's more powerful squadron, the French surrendered the island after a short bombardment. Curphy writes to his mother, brothers and sisters in the Isle of Man:

> I was turned over from the *Salamander* fireship October the 17th to the *Prince Edward* forty gun ship and were oblig'd to sail the next day to the Coast of guiney, to a place called the Island of goree, to take it, which we did on the 29th day of December with some small loss from the french, which we expect some prize money for very soon. But we took a french ship comeing home, which we expect to receive about twenty pounds a man for. She is richly laden from St Damingo a letter of Mark and only our own ship's company to share it for we parted all the rest of the fleet about a week before we took her. [I] Rcvd no money from the *Salamander* but we expect to receive it before the ship saile again from Portsmouth I wrote a letter at goree and sent it to you. Pray let me know whether you rcvd it or not last December, and pray write to me as speedy as you can direct to me on board the *Prince Edward* manawar at Portsmouth or elsewhere commanded by Captain William Fortisque.

Curphy goes on to describe the fate of a fellow Manx sailor, who probably died from a tropical disease:

> I am very sorry for haveing it to let you know that Ewan Garret is dead, which devise you will let his mother know. He died the 25th day of January last upon the coast of guiney. He had about one pound sixteen shills in money when he died ... which I got when he died and the officer took it from me and keeps it until farther directions from his mother, which I desire she will write to our Captain for it for me to get it to her and it shall be safe for her until I come home with it to her, which I hope will be very soon for there is a great many ships a paying off and I hope we shall not go out no more. So I shall write you for his will and power and receive his wages and bring it home to you. He was two years and five days in the King's Service and I know what he received of wages and what he got from the purser.
>
> I have got all the papers he had very safe and when I receive an answer from you I shall let you know in my next letter how much there is due to him. He first had a fever and then he took a flux which killed him tho' he was attended by three doctors. Pray mother, send me an answer and let me now what his mother or executors say to you. Remember my love to both William Christian and to my old neighbours all together. So no more at present from your loving and dutiful son William Curphy.[5]

The government of William Pitt the Elder pursued a successful policy in this war of preventing the French from engaging the British in home waters, by attacking them in their colonies and overseas possessions, and forcing the French to defend them. After the successful reduction of the fortress of Louisbourg, the way was prepared for the capture of Quebec, which would see French troops entirely driven out of Canada.

THE SEVEN YEARS' WAR

Prime Minister Pitt now decided to continue the strategy of taking the war to the enemy in their overseas possessions, by capturing France's Caribbean colonies. A key vessel in the Louisbourg campaign was the 74 gun warship HMS *Dublin*, one of the most modern in the Royal Navy at this time, based as she was upon the more advanced design of captured French war ships. She was now ordered south to the Leeward Islands, in order to engage French possessions there, and one of the sailors aboard her was John Lewin of Douglas. The West Indies were another unhealthy quarter of the globe and deaths from disease – particularly yellow fever – were rife among Royal Navy sailors there; at least one of his shipmates, a fellow Manxman, met his end this way. Some years later Lewin recounted his experiences, which were recorded by a court clerk in the Isle of Man:

> ... about nine years ago he ... was impressed into his Majesty's service in which service he continued till November last past. That about a year after this deponent was so impressed, as aforesaid which is now about eight years ago he ... was stationed on board one of his Majesty's ships of war called the *Dublin*. That about three or four years afterwards one Thomas Cubbon ... of Kirk Marown ... was also impressed, stationed & put on board the said ship of war the *Dublin*, where this deponent & he the said Thomas Cubbon continued till the latter end of the year one thousand seven hundred & sixty one or two but which this deponent is not positive of, during which time he, the said Thos Cubbon and the deponent, were very intimate, and this deponent further saith that he the said Thomas Cubbon being taken very ill sometime in the latter end of said years when the said ship of war *Dublin* was lying upon Fort Royal in the Island of Martinico, the said Thomas Cubbon was sent to the Kings Hospital in said Island to be taken care of till he had recovered. That after the said Thomas Cubbon was sent to the hospital as aforesaid, the ship of war the *Dublin* made a cruize off Highspaniola on which they

continued near three months after which they returned to Fort Royal, when & where this deponent made the strictest enquiry for his old friend acquaintances & country man the said Thomas Cubbon. And was there told by persons who belonged to said ship that were in said hospital at the same time that the said Thomas Cubbon was dead & buried about two or three weeks before their return which this deponent truely believes to be true.[6]

The Royal Navy in this era still had much to learn with regard to the links between cleanliness, diet, and the general health of its crews; as the century progressed this knowledge became more widespread within the navy, and deaths which were not directly attributed to battle declined significantly. In particular, the British naval surgeon James Lind discovered as early as 1753 that scurvy could be prevented by including citrus fruits in the diet, but the practice was not fully adopted by the Royal Navy until the 1790s. Although men suffered greatly in the war, women at home also had to shoulder a burden. When William Lace of Peel was impressed into the navy in December 1756, he was at first held in Stranraer gaol where, apprehensive of the fate which awaited him, he made out his will, two other Manxmen being his witnesses. His wife later stated that she had:

... laboured under great difficulties in supporting herself and child during near five years past her husband who was stationed on the coast of Jamaica being unable to send her any relief yet she with pleasure bore the burden in hopes of her said husbands return, but to [her] inexpressible grief she has of late received certain advice that her said husband dyed on board his Majesty's ship the *Enterprise*.[7]

It was not just the men who served below decks who were estranged from their families for long periods of time. Thomas Crebbin was one of the sons of the Reverend Paul Crebbin, vicar of Santon. During the Seven

THE SEVEN YEARS' WAR

Years' War Crebbin was in possession of a warrant as a surgeon, and Naval records indicate that he had held this position since 1757. By the time his father made his will some years later, Thomas had clearly been out of contact for a considerable length of time, for the Reverend Crebbin left him £100, reduced to 6d unless he returned to the Island or proved he was still alive by means of a letter. We catch a glimpse of Thomas Crebbin again after the close of hostilities, when he was surgeon aboard HMS *Deal Castle* stationed at New York, and he had probably been serving in American waters for some time. William Kneen of Ramsey meanwhile was impressed at Bowness in 1757, and was briefly held in Carlisle gaol along with several other Manx men. A touching letter survives which he wrote to his parents, who were clearly thinking of making the journey to Cumberland to try to have him freed. He writes:

> Honoured Father and Mother this is with my duty to you I am in good health at present god be thanked hopeing [sic] these few lines will find you the same so I beg you will keep good hearts & not fret yourselves about me because I want for nothing yet I received your letter febuary [sic] the 12th which grived [sic] me much because you would think to take such a jurney but after another maner I was very glad to hear of your welfare and is very glad that I received your letter. I sent a letter over to Peter Rume a week before I received your letter I sent over for two geeneys and to see if there was a pair of sockings left there and I got not answer out of it ... I desire that you will not let yourselves want for anything if there is any of mine to any service to you mony or anything else so I desire that you will take care of [my] Bills there is in my Chist and in a box behind my bed and in my Cointing Book so I give my father power to get what money belongs to me ... I want for nothing neither meat drink washing or bed and I desire that you will not send anything over to me because I do not expect to be here but a short time because there

is a Captain of a manawar com from new Castle for us which came in the yard to view us and tould us that we was to go away to new Castle the 17 of feb I desire my Service to all the Boat Crew.

One of the other men that he was with apparently could not write, and a court clerk in the Isle of Man later recorded that:

He was writing home to his friends & asked whether [he] had any [message] and that [Kneen] answered I desire my love & service to my wife (in Manx whereas they spoke Chorp as slaiynt gys my ven)...[8]

Shortly afterwards Kneen and some other men were posted to HMS *Rose* off the coast of North America, where he became ill and was placed in a hospital at Halifax, Nova Scotia; here he died and was buried. The story however tells us much about Manx sailors at this time – many seem to have been bilingual and some probably spoke little English, only Manx. It would seem likely that the Royal Navy kept Manx sailors together in groups, for then there would be a good chance that at least one could speak some English and could interpret for the others if necessary.

The war came directly to the shores of the Isle of Man in 1760, following the raid launched by French privateer Captain François Thurot on the Irish coast. Thurot was born at Nuits-St-Georges, near Dijon in 1727. His early life had been eventful, as following the death of his father he went to sea, firstly aboard a privateer, and subsequently as a smuggler around the coast of Ireland. The outbreak of the Seven Years' War had seen him appointed as an officer in the French *Marine Royale,* on the basis of his skills as a sailor, and he was quickly promoted to command a squadron of ships preying on shipping around the coasts of Britain and Ireland. However, his second commission would be his last. With a strong force intended to act as a diversion for a planned French invasion of England, he set off first for Scandinavia. On the way bad weather and leaked intelligence combined to deplete his force. By the time they reached Ireland the three surviving ships were low on morale and provisions. Their final huzzah was a raid on Carrickfergus, after which a British squadron from Dublin was ordered to intercept the Frenchmen.

Thurot's squadron was eventually brought to book by a force under Captain John Elliott of the Royal Navy at the Battle of the Point of Ayre, at which the former was decisively beaten. Elliott's squadron consisted of HMS *Aeolus, Pallas,* and *Brilliant,* that of Thurot comprising *Belleisle, Terpsichore,* and *La Blonde.* This small action was fiercely fought, and it contains as much drama as some better known engagements of this era; whilst there are several accounts of the course of the battle, that of Elliott himself is frustratingly brief:

> On the 28th [February], at four in the morning, we got sight of them, and gave chase. About 9 I got up alongside their Commodore (off the Isle of Man) and in a few minutes after the action became general, and lasted about an hour and a half, when they all three struck their colours; they are the *Marshal Belleisle* of 44 guns and 545 men, including troops, M.Thurot Commander, who is killed, the *La Blonde*, of 32 guns and 400 men, commanded by Captain La Kayce; and the *Terpsichore*, of 26 guns and 300 men, commanded by Capt. Defrauaudais. I put into this road to repair the ships, who are all much disabled in their masts and rigging, the *Marshal Belleisle* in particular, who lost her bowsprit, mizzen-mast, and main-yard in the action; and it was with great difficulty that we prevented her sinking. It is with the greatest pleasure I acquaint their Lordships, that the Officers and men of his Majesty's ships behaved remarkably well on this occasion.[9]

The French prizes were taken in tow – the *Belleisle* being in such a shattered condition that she had 5 feet of water in the hold when she struck her colours – and were taken to Ramsey Bay. A sailor who went to London with the express from Elliott's fleet affirmed that Thurot fought and was killed dressed like a sailor in an ordinary blue jacket – it was supposed the better to disguise himself, though this information must have comefrom French eyewitnesses as Thurot's body did not wash up on the Scottish coast until some days after the battle. Bishop Mark Hildesley famously witnessed at least some of the action from Bishopscourt, and wrote afterwards to his friend the Reverend Philip Moore:

> [Hearing of] Mons. Thurot's invasion, in Ireland, and being so near as to be almost within sight or hearing – we were in some doubt of the validity of the report – Till we were amply and sensibly resolved, by what passed but a little way from us yesterday morning – and what that was, you have by this time no need of my relation, on paper, as you will e'er now have had more than enough of personal description from the numbers that have been to wait on Thurot's remains at the sea-camp at Ramsey.[10]

People had hurried and flocked from all parts of the Island to observe the scene presented by the battle damaged ships in Manx waters, and an eye witness writes:

> On receipt of the news of Thurot being brought into Ramsey Bay on Thursday, last night, I went there to see the ships, etc. at daylight. I got on board the *Belleisle*, and was struck with astonishment; turn which way I would nothing but scattered limbs of dead and dying men presented themselves to my view, the decks and ship's sides could be compared to nothing but a slaughter-house; the English not having time to clear the vessel the night before, near 200 men being killed on board her, besides what the other two French ships lost. Thurot's body was thrown, by mistake, overboard amongst the rest. The French must have plundered all before them at Carrickfergus,

for I saw one of them stript who had eight women's shifts on him. They had plenty of women and children's shirts, caps, ruffles, shoes, petticoats, stays, bed curtains, sheets, buttons, thimbles, pins, bleached and grey yarn.[11]

Captain Elliott placed some of his men, who were dangerously wounded, on shore in Ramsey under the care of a local surgeon named Thomas Gillespie, but the representatives of the Duke of Atholl resolutely refused permission to land the prisoners on the Island, so as soon as the vessels were sufficiently repaired to undertake a sea voyage, the fleet set sail again. Before doing so, Captain Elliott held a ball aboard HMS *Aeolus* whilst she lay in Ramsey Bay. Here, Hester and Mary Heywood, daughters of Thomas Heywood of the Nunnery just outside Douglas, met their future husbands, then serving as midshipmen aboard the *Aeolus*. Mary married Thomas Pasley, who would figure prominently in Manx naval matters, and Hester married James Holwell, later to become a colonel of marines. Thomas Heywood's son was Peter John Heywood, a rising star under the Atholl regime, and one of the most important figures on the Isle of Man. At the age of just 25 he had been appointed Deemster by the Duke. Later, he would take on the role of Seneschal, the Duke's representative on the Island, yet his fall from grace would see him lose the Nunnery, perhaps the finest private house on the Island. Among his children were Hester ('Nessy') born in 1768 and Peter, born in 1772.

Despite the war, Manx slave ship captains were frequent visitors to the Island. We have evidence for the activities of a Manx-crewed vessel from a letter issued in 1762 by a Liverpool merchant to a Captain Lace, possibly also Manx, of the ship *Marquis of Granby* which states:

> With the First Favourable wind you must sail and proceed in company with the *Douglas*, Captain Finch, who has some Business at the Isle of Man, when you must accompany him not waiting longer for him than six days. When finished at the Isle of Man, you are to make the Best of your way in

Company thro the So. Channell and as you are Both Ships of Force, and we hope Tolerably well mann'd you will be better able to Defend yourselves against the Enemy, we therefore Recommend your keeping a good Look out that you may be Prepaird against an attack, and shoud you be Fortunate enough to take any vessell or vessells From the Enemy, we recommend your sending them Home or to Cork whichever will be most convenient so as not to Distress your own ship, and on your arrival at Old Callebar if one or more ships be there you will observe to make an agreement with the Master or Masters so as not to advance the Price on each other and we doubt not you will use your utmost endeavours to keep down the Comeys which in Generall are to extravagant there and For which you have no Return at least not worth any thing to the Ownery and as your Cargoe is larger than we expected we hope will be able to Purchase 550 slaves, and may have to spare £400 to lay out in Ivory which we Recommend your Purchasing From the Beginning of your Trade and pray mind to be very Choice in your Slaves.[12]

Issuing letters of marque to slave vessels was also a common practice at this time, and many of these ships combined the roles of slave trader and privateer. Not surprisingly, Liverpool was one of the principal ports from which such vessels were equipped and operated.

That year France managed to persuade Spain to join the war on her side, but British naval superiority was soon to bring the Seven Years' War to an end. The Spanish suffered heavy defeats and the loss of several significant colonial possessions; the French meanwhile simply could not counter the Royal Navy's global reach, and its ability to provide supplies and men both to Britain's forces in America, and to her allies in Europe. The British were able to deliver blows against French possessions in Canada and the West Indies, and at the same time disrupt French naval attempts to land her forces in the British Isles. With her income from trade cut off by the war, and with enormous military commitments in Europe to sustain, France was by now bankrupt, and sued for peace in 1763. However the Isle of Man was not to enjoy unfettered and unmolested trade as a result. The Governor advised the Duke of Atholl in June of that year that with the advent of peace, the government had more seamen available to it than it now needed, and so it had used them to augment the Revenue Service whose cutters greatly annoyed commercial shipping. The Douglas merchants for their part viewed things stoically, believing that the coming of both peace and war tended to disrupt trade, but that it was only a temporary situation.

It was to be only two more years however before another blow fell upon them, even more injurious to the Island's commerce than the recent war. For many years the British Parliament had sought to close the tax loophole which the Isle of Man represented. Now, following the Seven Years' War, the Westminster government was heavily in debt and sought to recoup revenue wherever it could. Various estimates showed that the loss to the exchequer through duties paid on goods landed in the Isle of Man came to something in the region of £350,000 a year. In addition, the brazen nature of the smugglers was an affront to His Majesty's customs. If the revenue cutters were small, they were often fired upon from the vessels heading to the coast of Scotland from the Isle of Man. If the cutters were larger, and managed to intercept them, the smugglers would simply dump their cargo in the sea, in the knowledge that they need only land a small quantity successfully to be in profit. Once ashore the contraband was quickly divided among mounted men, who disappeared rapidly into the rough country of the English borderlands. Again, violence and firearms were often used if they were intercepted.

Attempts had been made in the past by the Crown to reach agreement with the Duke of Atholl over the sale of his rights, but these had come to nothing. The second Duke, John Murray, had been old and in poor health, but when he died and his nephew James inherited the title, the British government let it be known that patience was running out. If he would not agree to sell, then his rights would be arbitrarily removed from him by Act of Parliament. The blow which had been feared for a generation finally came in 1765, when the third Duke agreed to sell. In the Act of Revestment the Crown purchased the regalities of the Isle of Man (i.e. the right to impose and collect taxes) but left the Atholls with Manorial rights, and therefore with some interests still in the Island. The negotiations with the Duke had been carried out in secret, and when the news of the impending Act broke, there was little time to do anything about it. The House of Keys sent a deputation to Westminster, however it arrived too late to be heard in Parliament. Interestingly, when the Act reached the Isle of Man, and copies were posted, it was suddenly apparent that hardly anyone could read it. A Manx translation was hastily prepared, and the result was uncertainty and alarm across the Island. Among the merchant class there was a minor panic. They were given six months to dispose of what they were holding, or pay duty upon it. Many traders, fearing a crash, sold up, and the resulting recession lasted several years.

The most obvious outward sign of the new regime was the presence in Manx harbours of British customs officers, searching for contraband; but as well as customs agents, the 1770s brought many naval officers to the Isle of Man. These men came as part of the coastal service, protecting the ports and harbours in the Irish Sea and on occasion pursuing suspicious craft on the old smuggling routes between Ireland and the Isle of Man. Many chose to settle on the Island for longer or shorter periods, and one such was Peter Fannin. He was born around 1735, probably in Ireland, and was well educated, being able to read and write clearly. Fannin had been a Master in the Royal Navy since 1760; the position at this time was that of senior Warrant Officer aboard a ship – the Master was in effect answerable only to the captain. Apart from a slight hiccup in 1760, when he was court martialled and dismissed from the sloop HMS *Wolf* after running the ship aground, Fannin had an exemplary career. He made his name as a seafarer in the Caribbean, as Master of the bomb ship HMS *Basilisk* off Jamaica and Martinique, and later in the same office aboard HMS *Richmond* also in the West Indies. He was meticulous in his descriptions of the anchorages which he came to, recording the depths of water to be found in various bays and inlets at Jamaica and elsewhere, as well as visual references.

In 1770 he was aboard the cutter HMS *Ferret* at Dublin, on coastal duties in the Irish Sea, and by 1771 he was Master of the cutter HMS *Garland,* also apparently operating in these waters. For the ships of the Royal Navy patrolling the seas around the Isle of Man it was a year-round task, and the weather in these waters could be unforgiving. In November 1771, Lieutenant James Norman, commanding the *Ferret*, reported from Douglas that:

> ... being at anchor under the island of Lambay, watching the motion of two smuggling cutters in Rush Harbour, and it blowing fresh; the gale increasing, endovered [sic] to weigh, the cable parted, lost the anchor and 48 fathom of cable; on the day following laying too of the Calf of Man, shipped a Great sea which filled the Cutter waist full and water log'd [sic] her; was obliged for the safety of the vessel and the preservation of our lives to cut away and throw overboard the cross jack yard sail top gallant mast out of the crutches and two of the cutter's logs to lighten her. Several other articles washed overboard at same time.[13]

Among the other Royal Navy ships based at Douglas at various times was HMS *Ranger,* the first commander of which after the Act of Revestment had been Captain Thomas Pasley. Later this sixty-man sloop was commanded by Captain John Henshaw. At other times the *Carcass* sloop, under Captain Skeffyn Lutwidge, the *Cholmondley* cutter under Lieutenant Halley Borwick, the *Lurcher* under Lieutenant William Long, and the cutter *Esther*, under Lieutenant John Baird undertook patrol work out of Douglas harbour. Some of the crews employed were less than satisfactory, Borwick in writing to the Admiralty asking for a new

Surgeon's Mate, added that Charles Smyth, the current holder of the post aboard the *Chomondley* was:

> ...an idle, worthless, drunken man and has been absent six weeks without leave with his [medicine] chest.[14]

Smyth had previously complained about the location of his medicine chest as being detrimental to the medicines within, despite the fact that it had stood in the same place for the previous six years. Borwick died whilst on service in the Isle of Man in 1770 and was buried at Braddan churchyard, whilst the following year the Surgeon's Mate of the *Esther,* Henry Allingham, also died and was buried in the same location. He was replaced by James Rose, Surgeon's Mate of the *Ranger*. Another naval officer, Lieutenant William Lockhart, a subsequent commander of the *Ferret,* gives us an insight into some of the tricks used by both poachers and gamekeepers on this station:

> You will observe from the Certificate ... of the Carpenter's expense for the Cutter I command, an exception to the use of soap mixt with Tallow for Paying the Cutter's Bottom, when on my station, as being an unusual composition in the Navy. I therefore thought it requisite to give you my reasons for using it, and I flatter myself you will approve of them. At the Isle of Man where I have hitherto gleaned the Butter and Soap and Tallow are generally of one Price or nearly so, the first of which is plenty and the latter but scarce, and as I found that a composition of that sort was always made use of by the vessels in that part of the World who are on the Revenue Service as being the Most Durable, I was therefore Encouraged to make use of it, and the more so as it did not bring any additional charge on the Government other than the Tallow alone would have done, and I will take it upon me to assert that it lasts double the time when mixt in that manner.[15]

THE SEVEN YEARS' WAR

Treating the hull of a vessel in this fashion made it smoother and also inhibited the growth of weeds, both of which made it faster in the water, though in the case of the *Ferret*, her commander's reports on the amount of bilge in her hold also make it clear that she was an ageing, leaky vessel. Captain James Jones, commander of the *Ferret* in 1771, wrote to the Admiralty in March of that year to complain that the incessant rain in the Isle of Man would destroy his sails, as at that time he had nowhere to store them when unbent. The previous storehouse which had been used by the Royal Navy cutters in Douglas had been sold by its owner. The following year Joseph Drury, formerly surgeon on board the *Ranger* was discharged due to ulceration of the lungs. Her captain felt that it was unwise to put to sea without a medical officer on board, and it seems that shortly afterwards Drury was replaced by James Hillyar, a surgeon from Portsmouth. Two of Hillyar's sons would subsequently join the navy and both became admirals, his son James in particular would become a friend of Lord Nelson and fought alongside him. The biography of the younger James records that he was first taken to sea by his father following the death of his mother, and it is tempting to think that the boy, 3 or 4 years of age, might have spent time in the *Ranger* in the waters off Douglas.

The presence of the Royal Navy in Douglas harbour must have made up to some extent for the loss of revenue due to the clampdown on the running trade. In addition to the many sailors who would undoubtedly have spent their pay in the inns and taverns on the town's quayside, we find many vouchers in the naval records for maintenance work undertaken on vessels by Douglas shipwrights, particularly Matthias Kelly, and also for ship's stores purchased from chandlers such as John Taylor or John Gelling. Local sailors also received wages when acting as pilots for Royal Navy ships. Peter Fannin came to the Isle of Man with the navy, but also chose to make his home in Douglas.

It was around this time that he came to the attention of the legendary explorer Captain James Cook, who was then planning his second voyage to the Pacific. Cook had two ships on this expedition, HMS *Resolution* and HMS *Adventure*, and had carte blanch to hand pick his crews. It is a testament to Fannin's ability as a navigator that Cook had appointed him as Master of the *Adventure*, a barque 100 feet in length with a crew of eighty and eighteen guns. It was a position with responsibility for the handling of the ship, and directly below that of the Captain Tobias Furneaux, another highly experienced explorer.

As part of Cook's second expedition *Resolution* and *Adventure* left Plymouth on 13 July 1772, and on 17 January of the following year were the first European ships to cross the Antarctic Circle. On 8 February 1773 the two ships became separated in a fog, and Furneaux directed *Adventure* towards the prearranged meeting point of Queen Charlotte Sound, New Zealand, previously charted by Cook in 1770. On the way to the rendezvous, *Adventure* surveyed the southern and eastern coasts of Tasmania (then known as Van Diemen's Land), where Adventure Bay was named after the ship. After calling at Tahiti and Tonga *Adventure* set out for home on 22 December 1773 via Cape Horn.

Before she did so, there was a shocking incident in Queen Charlotte Sound, in which Peter Fannin was directly involved. Relations with the local Maori people appeared hostile from the start, with several confrontations between them and the British seamen. As the ship was re-supplying ready for the long voyage home, her crew gathered as much fresh water, firewood and food as they could reasonably accommodate. On the night of 17 December, Furneaux sent one of the ship's boats in search of fresh greens. When she had not returned by next morning he grew concerned and sent another party, more heavily armed, in search of the first. It was under the command of the Second Lieutenant, Burney, and the Master, Peter Fannin. Although no account in Fannin's own words has survived, Burney's personal log has, and it provides a graphic account of what transpired. Coming to a native settlement by the water's edge, Burney writes:

> We went ashore and searched the canoe, where we found one of the rullock ports of the cutter, and some shoes, one of which was known to belong to Mr Woodhouse one of our

midshipmen. One of the people at the same time brought me a piece of meat, which he took to be some of the salt meat belonging to the cutter's crew. On examining this and smelling it I found it was fresh. Mr Fannin who was with me, supposed it was dog's flesh, and I was of the same opinion; for I still doubted their being cannibals. But we were soon convinced by most horrid and undeniable proof. A great many baskets lying on the beach tied up, we cut them open. Some were full of roasted flesh and some of fern root, which serves them for bread. On farther search, we found more shoes, and a hand, which we immediately knew to have belonged to Thomas Hill, one of our fore-castle men, it being marked T.H. with an Otaheite tattow-instrument.

On rounding the next bay, which was called Grass Cove, they saw four canoes and a number of natives, which they scattered with a volley of musketry. Burney continues:

I then landed with the marines, and Mr Fannin stayed to guard the boat. On the beach were two bundles of cellery, which had been gathered for loading the cutter. A broken oar was stuck upright in the ground, to which the natives had tied their canoes; a proof that the attack had been made here. I then searched all along at the back of the beach to see if the cutter was there. We found no boat, but instead of her such a shocking scene of carnage and barbarity as can never be mentioned or thought of but with horror, for the heads, hearts and lungs of several of our people were seen lying on the beach, and, at a little distance, the dogs gnawing their intrails. While we remained almost stupified on the spot, Mr. Fannin called to us that he heard the savages gathering together in the woods; on which I returned to the boat, and hauling alongside the canoes we demolished three of them...

The party continued along the coast, hoping to find the missing cutter but only finding more evidence of warlike natives; at the same time they were aware that they were heavily outnumbered, and that in any enterprise ashore they would have to leave about half their number to guard their own boat. Burney goes on:

> I consulted with Mr Fannin, and we were both of the opinion that we could expect to reap no other advantage than the poor satisfaction of killing some more of the savages. At leaving Grass Cove, we had fired a general volley towards where we heard the Indians talking; but by going in and out of the boat, the arms had got wet, and four pieces missed fire. What was still worse, it began to rain; our ammunition was more than half expended; and we left six large canoes behind us in one place. With so many disadvantages, I did not think it worth while to proceed, where nothing could be hoped for but revenge.[16]

On his charts, Fannin referred to Grass Cove as 'Bloody Bay' in reference to the massacre. HMS *Adventure* reached England on 14 July 1774 and entered the Royal Dockyard at Deptford. Peter Fannin almost immediately returned to the Isle of Man and was married at Braddan church in March of 1775. His bride was Elizabeth Booth, the daughter of George Booth, who founded the Douglas brewery which would later become known as Clinch's.

Also on the Isle of Man at this time was a young man who would go on to become one of the best known figures in British naval history. William Bligh, the 21-year-old son of a parson from Plymouth, was now on board the Royal Navy cutter HMS *Ranger* stationed at Douglas. He was listed on the ship's books as 'AB' (Able Seaman) but in fact was regarded as a First Class Volunteer, a young gentleman with aspirations to become an officer, who messed and quartered with the midshipmen.

In April 1775, whilst Bligh was with the ship, another young man was recorded in the books in the same capacity, Robert Benjamin Young.

THE SEVEN YEARS' WAR

He was apparently born in Douglas and was the son of the ship's Master, Robert Parry Young. His mother, formerly Jane Redfern, was from a Manx family and lived at Castletown prior to her marriage. However, there is some hint of scandal here, for according to his later published biographies, Robert Benjamin would have been only 2 years old at this time. There is some suspicion that he was born out of wedlock, and the likely scenario is that he was actually around 10 years old when he joined the ship, but later modified his date of birth to make it more respectable. Bligh would get his first step on the promotion ladder later that year when he was advanced to Master's Mate aboard the *Ranger*. Master's Mate was not a position which would usually lead to a promotion to Master, but instead was regarded as a post which would provide experience for those hoping to be commissioned as a lieutenant. Bligh was later to take his lieutenant's examination and despite one or two infamous setbacks along the way, would eventually reach the rank of Vice Admiral. In contrast, mainly through lack of family influence, Robert Benjamin Young would find rising through the ranks of the Royal Navy frustratingly difficult, in spite of his undoubted bravery.

The Master of the *Ferret*, Alexander Cheyne, died in 1774 apparently in Douglas, whilst in 1776, when the *Esther* was without a Master, her commander Lieutenant Christopher Mayer wrote to the Admiralty for permission to appoint Robert Spiney, previously Master's Mate in HMS *Lark* and *Ranger* and now resident in Douglas, to the position. Another officer who served aboard the *Esther* around this time was Lieutenant Benjamin Bechinoe, who had also sailed with James Cook early in his career, being third lieutenant aboard HMS *Pembroke* in 1759, at the same time as Cook had been aboard as Master. Bechinoe, like many other officers must have had a family home on the Isle of Man, for in 1775 his young son died, and was buried in Onchan churchyard. It seems likely that Peter Fannin knew most of these men from his time in the coastal service (indeed it is possible that it was Bechinoe who recommended him to Cook). He was later to establish a school of navigation in Douglas, training a new generation of Manxmen for life at sea, and he seems to have been greatly respected. The Reverend Philip Moore, in 1780 wrote to the Curate of Kirk Michael:

> This will be delivered to you by Mr Fanning, one of the great circumambient navigators, who is come to take an elevation of good Bishop Wilson's tomb in your churchyard ... You will be so good as to show Mr Fanning the tomb, and for the few hours that he may be imployed and to shew him such civility as is due to such a worthy man in all civilised nations.[17]

In his later years Fannin seems often to have been in financial difficulty, and was taken to court on a number of occasions for petty debts. However his skills as a cartographer were impressive, for in semi-retirement some years later he went on to draw up a map of the Isle of Man, apparently on behalf of the Duke of Atholl. As an inset it contains one of the earliest street plans of Douglas. It is believed that Fannin worked on the map at the merchant Robert Black's old house. Latterly the house was owned by the Duke of Atholl, who gave the lease to his Seneschal, Peter John Heywood. After the deaths of Heywood and his widow, the Duke lived there intermittently until Castle Mona was completed. The theory is given credence by the fact that Fannin included the view across the harbour from the Duke of Atholl's house as an inset.

The second half of the eighteenth century was one in which it seemed that commerce and war were inextricably bound together; indeed the one drove the other, for it was the expanding trade of Great Britain which brought her into increasing conflict with her European rivals over colonial possessions. Growing trade, and the need to protect it from foreign powers, led at the same time to increasing British naval strength. Britain emerged from the Seven Years' War as a major world power, having thwarted the colonial ambitions of her nearest rival, France, in the Americas and in the East Indies, and with a Royal Navy which had grown enormously in terms of size, strength and professionalism. With the coming of peace, colonial ambition combined with scientific curiosity led the Royal Navy to begin an era of epic journeys to the then farthest known parts of the planet, and to begin to fully map Australia and the Pacific. This however was also an age of new ideas and original political thinking. There was a growing awareness and understanding of science for example. With this came largely for the first time the questioning of authority (particularly that derived from supernatural sources, such as religious teaching).

Also for the first time, in the 1770s, a British colony would feel able to challenge the dominance of rule from London. The ideas which gave rise to the American Revolution still have resonance today, but they would profoundly shake the established European order in the years which followed. For the Isle of Man, although its trade had suffered a grievous blow in 1765, and its wealth and status had been diminished as a result, the expansion of the last decades of the century offered the prospect of new opportunities for its people, whose skills as seafarers in particular would be in growing demand.

Chapter 2

The American War

In many ways the Seven Years' War directly begat the American War of Independence. Some of Great Britain's colonies in North America, freed as they were from the threat of foreign colonial powers (particularly that from the French), now felt emboldened to challenge what they saw as the injustices of punitive taxation and rule from far distant London. At the same time the cost of the Seven Years' War had left Great Britain heavily in debt. The British Parliament felt that taxes were already high enough at home, and believed the American colonists should bear some of the cost of the military formations stationed there for their defence. They imposed taxation upon them in March 1765 (around the same time that the Act of Revestment was introduced against the Isle of Man), to the outrage of the colonists, who protested that they were not represented at Westminster, and thus had no say over how taxes were raised or spent.

After the Boston Tea Party, when a group dressed as native Americans threw a cargo of tea into the harbour, the British government tried to exert direct control in Massachusetts; the colonists in turn began to arm, and formed a Provincial Congress. Negotiations over tax arrangements were still going on between Congress and Parliament when hostilities broke out in 1775. From 1776, Bourbon France (eager for revenge upon Britain after its defeat in 1763) had been informally involved in the war, after the American statesman Thomas Jefferson sought a French alliance. With supplies and weapons from this source reaching the United States, it would not be long before matters escalated further into all-out war between Britain, France, Spain and Holland.

The immediate impact of the American Revolutionary War upon the people of the Isle of Man came from the efforts of the Royal Navy to

THE AMERICAN WAR

bolster its manpower, by recruiting sailors. Sometimes the Manx people found themselves the victim of violent press gangs of naval men who came ashore looking for victims, or the crews of privateers authorised to seize enemy ships were the aggressors. On 5 November 1776, Richard McNally, of Douglas, alleged that Captain Smith, the master of a private sloop then in Douglas harbour, came with his crew into an inn where he and a friend were drinking, and attacked them with swords and cutlasses:

> Such was the madness of the said persons, that they struck one of their swords upon your petitioner's head, and stole or took away his wig.[18]

Most vulnerable to impressment were the crews of merchant ships. These experienced men who knew how to set a sail, could climb rigging on a pitching ship and who had hauled ropes were the navy's ideal targets. Press gangs were supposed only to take seamen, but such was the urgent requirement for men that almost anyone would do. On one occasion in 1777, Stephen Brew, a shoemaker from Douglas was impressed by the cutter HMS *Esther* in Douglas harbour, and carried off with her to Portsmouth. Here and at other major ports the ships of the Royal Navy were readying themselves for war. New recruits, willing or unwilling, came aboard along with stores and ammunition. One of these vessels was HMS *Raisonnable* a 64-gun third-rate ship of the line, named after a French vessel captured in the previous war, lying at Plymouth. Among the 500 or so officers and men on board were 8 Manx sailors. History does not record if they were impressed (though this seems likely) but we do know that two brothers from Marown were serving together, Thomas and John Gale, both of whom were rated as Landsmen. The former wrote to their mother Barbara in March 1777, telling her:

> I take this opportunity of writing these two or three lines to you hoping to find you in good health as I am now at Present thanks be to god for it and to Let you know of your son John.

We are both together on the same ship which is called the *Raisonable* [sic] We are in good health thank god but you come in our thoughts how you com on a tom [sic] We met with William Cottier sholdor [soldier] from Kirk Marown and he is as harty as can be but he would sooner come home than stay ... abord the ship that is called the *Ocean* and I believe she goes along with us but how soon she sails we cant tell at present or where she is bound to but shall let you have the satisfaction of knowing as soon as possible We never Received no money yet but we expect it Every Day Now Dear mother we conn [?] for Inglish Very Well We Don't Want for nowat neither so no more at present from your Dutyfull sons.[19]

The last sentence seems to imply possibly that the Gales spoke mainly Manx at home, but could make themselves understood in the navy. The *Raisonnable* sailed for the American colonies not long afterwards, but the two brothers died before they saw active service. Word must have reached their mother, for Barbara Gale enlisted the help of Douglas surgeon Dr Patrick Scott to write to the Office of the Navy to enquire after her sons. The rather unhelpful clerk who replied complained of being overworked, but confirmed that the two men were indeed dead and that their mother could claim their arrears of wages. That was provided she obtained an administration from the Prerogative Court in London, and a parish certificate being presented to show that she was indeed their mother and 'a person of good character'. One wonders if she ever received the money.

The British Army, which had abandoned Boston, went on to take New York from the colonials, and the British held the city as a base for operations further afield until the end of the war. It was also the site of hospitals and sick quarters for the Royal Navy, and at least one Manx sailor, William Crow of Onchan (who had been aboard HMS *Terrible)* is recorded as having passed away here. Later in the summer of 1777, the British began the Saratoga campaign, an attempt to seize control of the

THE AMERICAN WAR

Hudson Valley in the state of New York. However British troops from New York City failed to link up with those which had advanced south from Quebec, and the campaign ended in disaster.

After learning of the American victory at Saratoga, the French became concerned that the British would now reconcile their differences with the colonists and turn on France. In particular, the French King Louis XVI was influenced by alarmist reports suggesting that Britain was preparing to make huge concessions to the colonies and then, allied with them, strike at French and Spanish possessions in the West Indies. Previously the French had limited their assistance to the Americans to clandestine military aid and advice. In order to thwart any Anglo-American rapprochement, on 6 February 1778, they concluded a formal treaty of alliance with the United States, committing the Americans to seek nothing less than absolute independence. Previously France had only been willing to act in conjunction with her ally Spain, which was not yet ready to become formally involved in the conflict, but now she was prepared to go to war alone if necessary. Britain responded by recalling its ambassador in Paris, and in March 1778 the French ambassador was withdrawn from London, although Franco-British hostilities did not actually break out until June of that year.

Almost from the outset of the war the people of the Isle of Man had also been greatly affected by the numbers of American warships which infested the Irish Sea. The future United States president, Benjamin Franklin, at that time in France, wrote that he had no doubt that one or two frigates operating in Britain's coastal waters would have a disproportionate effect upon her maritime trade, and so it proved. Three small American cruisers, *Lexington*, *Reprisal* and *Dolphin* made two complete circuits of Ireland, capturing several prizes and bringing them into European ports to sell in order to raise funds for Congress. Their actions caused panic and alarm among the merchants of Great Britain, who demanded Royal Navy protection for their ships not only on far distant routes, but for vessels importing linen on the short journey from Ireland to England. One observer noted that in no previous war, in none of the conflicts with France or Spain, had protection been demanded for ships in the Irish Sea. The United States however lacked a large formal navy, and thus also placed great reliance upon privateers. The Reverend Philip Moore had tried to reassure a friend in July 1777 by telling him:

> Be quiet and never mind these American rovers. The likes of you and I have nothing to fear from the likes of them. Let the rich fat ransomers look to themselves – they that have nothing to lose, can nothing lose, Our friend at Andreas [Archdeacon Mylrea] talks of being murdered in our beds, I wonder what should put that into his head. For these Buccaneers have murdered nothing – but a few ships that I can hear of. They would much rather I believe meet with some of your linen fleet – for I fancy the poor devils many of them, may want a shirt to their backs.[20]

The situation was about to become much more serious however with the arrival in these waters of the most celebrated American naval officer of this era, John Paul Jones, who commanded the USS *Ranger*. There can be no doubt that Jones would have been familiar with the seas around the Isle of Man, because the Douglas customs book recorded that the first cargo of rum landed there following the Act of Revestment was brought from England on a vessel commanded by him. Of Scots birth, John Paul (he added 'Jones' later, allegedly to throw creditors off his trail) started his maritime career at the age of 13, sailing out of Whitehaven as an apprentice. His older brother William had married and settled in Fredericksburg, Virginia, and this became the destination of many of the youngster's early voyages. For several years John Paul had sailed aboard a number of British merchant and slave ships, but after a short time in the latter business he became disgusted with the cruelty of the slave trade, and found other work. Upon the outbreak of war between the colonies and Great Britain, Paul chose to fight for his brother's adopted land.

THE AMERICAN WAR

Having crossed the Atlantic to France, *Ranger* sailed from Brest on 10 April 1778, bound for the Irish Sea and four days later captured a prize between the Scilly Isles and Cape Clear. On 17 April, she took another prize and sent her back to France. On 23 April Captain Jones led a daring raid on the port of Whitehaven, spiking the guns of the fortress and burning the ships in the harbour. This attack in particular caused much disquiet in the Isle of Man. Whenever suspicious sails were sighted off Douglas, the bellman was at once sent round the town to cry a proclamation that all persons having swords, guns, and pistols must forthwith assemble at the Fort 'to fight Paul Jones'. Tradition later had it that the invariable effect of this proclamation was suddenly to remind the majority of the menfolk of Douglas that they had pressing engagements in the countryside.

It was now on the seas as much as upon the land that this war would be decided. Put simply the British could afford to lose a few thousand soldiers, many of whom were German mercenaries, in the battles in New England but the war upon her maritime commerce was far more serious. Like the Americans and their French allies, the British Government proceeded to try to do as much injury as possible to enemy commerce by issuing 'letters of marque'. These permitted merchants and other owners to fit out armed ships, or privateers in order to attack enemy merchant vessels, and to retain a share of the value of ships or merchandise which they might capture. Effectively this was legalised piracy, the letter of marque protecting the captain from prosecution by confirming that he acted under the authority of his government. Privateers abounded during this conflict, in part at least because the war with the United States caused enormous disruption to the slave trade. Merchants in ports such as Liverpool found that there were considerable numbers of slave ships and their crews which were idle, and there was nothing else for it but to fit these out as privateers. Many of those Liverpool crews of course were Manx.

A group of merchants on the Isle of Man also thought that a venture of this nature would be a profitable one, and so they pooled their resources and purchased a ship called the *Tyger* for the sum of £3,465. The chief owners were Hugh Cosnahan and Lewis Geneste of Douglas, but according to a ballad of the time, a number of small investors and her captain, Richard Qualtrough also had a share in her. She had a crew of seventy men, twenty-five of whom were able seamen. One of the lieutenants was named Callister, the other was a John Moore. One of the petty officers was John Callow, who was subsequently master of the brig *Hope*. Of the able seamen, only the name of one is known in full, Harry Moore. The *Tyger* carried sixteen guns, fourteen of which were 6-pounders, and two 4-pounders. These were not the largest cannon in use at the time, but they nevertheless rendered the *Tyger* a formidable opponent to any vessel which was not a man-of-war. In December 1778, Captain Qualtrough wrote a letter, headed 'Tyger, Ramsey', to Lewis Geneste, in which he informed him of a planned cruise to the West Indies, and also of a failed attempt to seize a smuggler:

> ... alongside of which we were making ready to steal the next morning, and did not despair of taking possession of her from our own ship's height to command her decks, tho' she mounts 16 sixes, and 50 men, but she sailed that night. Should a similar incident occur, your orders shall be strictly complied with. We still find sufficient employment, but are now pretty ready, and wish for a fair wind. If convenient I will call in your bay (Douglas) by the way. The ship makes little or no water. I have given the sides a good coat of tar. The crew are pretty expert in their exercise and in good harmony. If it would be agreeable I would prefer calling at Montego Bay prior to Kingston, as at the latter place they would sweep away officers, seamen and all.[21]

This last remark refers to the all too frequent impressment of merchant seamen into the Royal Navy around that port. Qualtrough also suggested to Geneste that the crew should not be informed that their destination was Jamaica, because if they were, they would speedily 'make off'. On arriving off Land's End they encountered a terrible storm, but a few days later they captured the Dutch ship, *De Jonge Jessie Wittween de Lemmer*, under Captain Heere Anskes, bound from Bordeaux to Dieppe, loaded with 289 hogsheads of tobacco. After a quick run the *Tyger* and her prize arrived in Douglas, where they were greeted by the population with great joy. It was a joy, however, which was speedily turned into sorrow as the governor declared the capture an illegal one, the Dutch Republic at that time being still neutral.

He sent John Cosnahan, son of Hugh Cosnahan, representing the owners, together with Captain Anskes and three of his crew to Whitehaven, where they appeared before the Commissioners of the High Court of the Admiralty. An agreement was entered into between them and the commissioners that, on the owners of the *Tyger* paying £60 to Captain Anskes, and agreeing to put him and his crew once more in possession of his vessel, he should renounce any further claims against the owners of the *Tyger*. The Dutch captain remained in Douglas refitting till the middle of February, when he sent in his bill of costs for thirty days, amounting to £45 8s 8d, which was duly paid by Hugh Cosnahan. So ended the *Tyger*'s first unfortunate venture. We catch a glimpse of Captain Qualtrough again, briefly, in another letter from the Reverend Philip Moore in Whitehaven, dated 18 July 1779 and written in his usual eccentric style:

> You may, notwithstanding, be assured that a certain itinerant of no great note, nor of any consequence to anybody, but to himself and his friends, who are not a few, is now here, corporally, personally and identically well lodged, and kindly entertained at the house of Peter John Heywood, Esqre., who by virtue of the power in him vested – and by writ of habeas corpus seized this rambler – and secured him, bag and baggage as above. Said Itinerant here found the brave Capt. Qualtrough of the *Tyger* and Letter of Marque and Reprizal – about business best known to himself, and wish him success – intending to have taken my passage with him this day, and, like honest O'Blunder, to have been the bearer of this, myself.

But am sorry for the disappointment, as the nature of his business does not permit him to take in his recruits – if any he gets, here – but at Parton, which on many accts would be very inconvenient to me – beside – an open boat, and the chance, or rather mischance, of an attack from a large press-gang, lying in wait to intercept our Capt. and his men. A random shott, you know, on such an occasion, might spoil a man's coat, or make a hole in his doublet, which would not be very agreeable.[22]

Spain, eager to recover her lost territories of Florida, Menorca and especially Gibraltar, which had been ceded to Britain after previous conflicts, finally entered the war officially in June 1779, as an ally of France. Like their neighbour, the Spanish had been providing assistance to the American revolutionaries since the very beginning of the conflict. Now, her merchant ships would also become valid prizes of war if they could be captured. There is an interesting case of a far more successful privateer, albeit with a Manx master aboard an Irish vessel – Captain Thomas Moore, of the *Fame*, out of Dublin. She carried no less than twenty 6-pounder guns on one deck, with a further two 4-pounders and two 3-pounders on her quarter-deck. Her crew numbered some 108 men. There is a degree of uncertainty surrounding Moore's identity but he is generally associated with the Moores of Pulrose, and is believed to have been born in 1750 and died in 1808. One account of his actions comes from the British consul at Algiers, who states that Moore sailed from Mahon (in Menorca, then under British control) and upon receiving word soon after of the departure of five French vessels, all letters of marque from Marseilles, bound for the West Indies, he was determined to engage them. He captured four, off Cap de Gat:

> The largest ship, *Les Deux Freres*, pierced for 20 guns, mounting 14 six-pounders, and 55 men (fifteen of whom got off in a boat); the second *L'Univers*, (the captain of which was killed), pierced for 18 guns, carries 12 four-pounders and

THE AMERICAN WAR

41 men, little inferior in size to the *Deux Freres*; the third, the *Zephir*, (formerly His Majesty's sloop) pierced for 14 guns, mounting 10 three-pounders and 18 men; the fourth, the *Nancy*, a pink of 2 six-pounders, 2 two-pounders, and 18 men. They got all safe into this bay on the 29th of last month about 10 o'clock at night. Capt. Moor's gallant behaviour has been taken great notice of by the officers of this regency; and his humane and generous treatment of his prisoners been admired by every body; indeed so much so, that Mons. De la Vallee, French consul-general here, thought it incumbent upon him to write a line to me to express his sense of it in the strongest terms of encomium and gratitude.[23]

The career of this formidable vessel was not to last long however, for the *Belfast Newsletter* of 21 March 1780 states that the *Fame* of Dublin had been driven ashore by a French frigate, and had been totally destroyed along with the loss of a number of her crew. In later life, Captain Thomas Moore lived at Maghera-keu near Maughold. Meanwhile, in the summer of 1780 the owners of the *Tyger*, undaunted by their previous experience, commissioned her for a four month cruise. Three days out from Douglas she fell in with the British fleet under the command of Sir Charles Hardy, off the Scillies. She was brought too by HMS *Romney*, under Captain George Johnstone, who tried in vain to induce some of the crew to volunteer for the Royal Navy. On their refusal, he forcibly took all of the able seamen except one, who had been disabled by an accident, on board his own ship. It was reported later that Johnstone afterwards spoke of these men as the finest fellows he ever saw. Captain Qualtrough, however, having lost the pick of his crew, was unable to navigate the ship properly, and so returned to Douglas. This latest disaster proved too much for the owners, who now decided to sell the *Tyger*, and they parted with her for only £1,260, this being as much as they could get for her. However they attempted to recover some of their loss by means of a personal lawsuit against Captain Johnstone, when he returned to England in October 1780.

The ferocity and violence which was used by the Royal Navy in these acts made them more feared than the enemy by the merchant crews. In once incident, a merchant ship commanded by a Manxman named Crebbin was pursued by a frigate under the command of Captain James McNamara. When they were eventually overhauled, Crebbin was taken aboard the warship where McNamara struck him on the head with his speaking trumpet, using such force that he died from the blow. No wonder that men would do almost anything to get away. Hugh Crow, a Ramsey boy, grew up by the harbour and naturally wanted to go to sea as his career. He managed to obtain an apprenticeship with a merchant in Whitehaven, who looked kindly upon him and who paid for his education whenever he happened to be in port. Aged 17, Crow made his maiden sea journey around this time, heading first to Cork, and then on to the West Indies. He recounts how he first encountered the press gang, and the revulsion which it engendered within him:

> While at Cork, to our great vexation and inconvenience, all our best seamen were impressed. The scenes of oppression and distress which I witnessed every night, arising out of the cruel system of impressment, which is alike repugnant to liberty and to humanity, it is impossible for me adequately to describe. Some of the sailors, to escape the press-gang, leaped overboard, and swam from ship to ship, or endeavoured to gain the shore: others were in danger of being smothered by stowing themselves away in confined places below decks: and those who fell into the hands of the Philistines were dragged away like felons, sometimes by the hair of the head. Our captain, after much trouble and delay, succeeded in procuring fresh hands, and we sailed under convoy, with a fleet of between forty and fifty sail, bound to the island of Barbadoes.[24]

A merchant sailor who was less lucky, and who found himself forcibly enlisted into the Royal Navy at this time was John Gell, the son of

THE AMERICAN WAR

the Reverend Samuel Gell, Vicar of Lonan. When he was 7 years old, John was sent by his father to school in Douglas, to be taught by the Reverend Philip Moore, with whom he continued until he was 14 years of age. His father had a large family and a small income, so he could not afford to pay to have his son indentured to a tradesman. Instead, John was next sent to the school in Douglas run by Peter Fannin, by whom he was instructed in navigation, and at 16 years of age he was apprenticed to John Joseph Bacon, the merchant, to serve five years as a mariner on his ships. Gell relates an incident which occurred during his first journey:

> ... upon Monday evening, we sailed in a ship called the *Six Sisters*, bound to Barbadoes; on the Sunday following we fell in with a French privateer about two leagues off Cork, and after two hours' desperate engagement our ship was obliged to surrender, our ammunition being exhausted, and she was made a prize of by the enemy, and was ransomed for £1500, and one month allowed us to proceed on our voyage. Owing to severe weather and contrary winds, and our ship being much damaged, the month allowed us was expired before we arrived at our intended port, and we unfortunately fell in with a large Spanish fleet homeward bound from Buenos Ayres, and were again taken by them prisoners, and landed in Cadiz, in Spain, and then imprisoned during nineteen weeks and upwards, upon very short allowance. There happened at that time to be an exchange of prisoners, and we were marched, 240 in number, to Port Saint Lucas, a distance of many miles, and put on board of a Cartel bound to Portsmouth. When we arrived near to Cape Clear, in Ireland, we took by force possession of the Cartel (for which there is no law), and brought her into Douglas harbour, in the Isle of Man, where her captain and several of the exchanged prisoners died in a putrid fever.

A cartel was a merchant ship used for the exchange of prisoners, and regarded by both sides as neutral. Despite his experiences, the boy quickly returned to sea:

> Some few weeks afterwards I again sailed from Douglas in a large cutter, the property of the said merchant, Mr. Bacon, and bound to South Carolina, and within three leagues of that place we met with three American ships well armed, bound to France, and were by them taken prisoners and landed in Lorion, in France, and from thence marched to Donan prison, a distance of scores of miles, and there closely confined with hundreds of prisoners of different nations, nearly in a way of starvation, having very little to eat, and no beds, but merely a trifle of straw, without any covering but our own clothes, some of the prisoners dying daily, from eight to twelve in number. Nine weeks we remained in this deplorable situation, till to our great joy 200 of us were marched to a harbour called Saint Maloes and put on board a Cartel bound to Plymouth, and when we arrived there, near the king's ships lying at anchor, the night being uncommonly dark, four of us took the Cartel's small boat, and got on shore unnoticed, and, being young and able, we made the best of our way towards Liverpool, travelling by night, through fear of being seen and impressed, and keeping, in Hidlands the most part of the day.

Hidland was a Manx term for a hiding place specifically for avoiding a marauding press gang. There were supposedly a number on the Isle of Man. Gell's troubles were far from over however because whilst at an inn near Runcorn they were seized by a press gang from Liverpool. However, once outside, Gell and his comrades decided to fight:

> Two of them had cutlasses, and four of them bludgeons, and we with our sticks, until one of them had his arm broken, and

another desperately wounded in the head, and the rest sadly bruised by blows and falls. None of us were very much hurted excepting me, who received a cut in my head with a cutlass, which caused the blood to flow over my eyes and down my cheeks, that with difficulty I could see to hit my mark as I wished. Well battered and bruised, they at last made off, and our bloody engagement ended, leaving us the glory of the field. We then with all speed set out quite a contrary road, and concealed ourselves in a farmer's barn, by the farmer's liberty, until night, when he gave us a good supper, the only sufficient meal we had made use of during three weeks and more. The next morning he sent a man and horse with a letter from me to Mr. Leece, merchant in Liverpool, who sent for us to Liverpool in the night, and were put on board a Manx trader commanded by Edward Kegg of Castletown, and landed the day after in Derby Haven, when we were treated with great hospitality by Mr. Afflick and family, and he lent me his horse to ride to my father's in Kirk Lonon, as my head was so severely cut and bruised.[25]

This however brought Gell's seafaring career to a conclusion. With his parent's approval he returned to his schooling, Bacon having released him from his indenture.

A further iniquity of impressment was that those with money and influence could avoid it. Evidence of this comes from an incident which occurred in April 1780, when an employee of John Taubman called Thomas Stole was impressed by a Royal Navy gang, whilst on an errand to Lancaster taking a boat selling herrings. Not only was Stole confined in Lancaster Castle, but the master of the vessel had run away (despite the press gang offering fifteen shillings for information as to his whereabouts) leaving it in the sole care of a boy. Taubman made enquiries about the matter with Robert Parry Young (by now a Lieutenant), with whom he was acquainted socially through his friendship with the Redferns. The incident also serves to illustrate the close links which existed between Young (whose protégé of course was William Bligh) and the Taubmans (who were related by marriage to the Christians). Young replied from his ship HMS *Severn*, then at Liverpool:

> [your letter] gave me grate satisfaction to here from you the man you mention is now on board the Tender under my command as it so turns out of his being impressed I am glad his lott was to my Tender in consequence of which I assure you from your application and regard for the Island in General nothing shall be wanting on my side to use every effort I am master of to get your request complyed with. I only recommend to those connected or concerned with the man to have a little patience and in a short time I flatter myself with sending or landing him myself in the Island in the mean time he shall have every indulgence in my power more so than I grant in common had I not been favoured with yours I should not have come to the knowledge of the person you mention notwithstanding he having been on board the Tender for a fortnight pryor to my receipt of yours, and on my asking him why he did not make himself known to me. As for his reply that he was ashamed had he but have made himself known he should have been with you a long time since.

The difficulty now arose because HMS *Severn* was under orders to depart for Plymouth, and Young warned Taubman that he thought he could do nothing to get the man released until they reached that port. Young's next letter, reporting that Stole had indeed been released, was carried personally back to Taubman, though it seems this was not accomplished without some bribery being necessary:

> I have the satisfaction to say after very grate intervention that I embrace this opportunity by the man himself whome

I have got discharged unserviceable some small expenses have attended but very modest I am happy at any rate to think I have accomplished this matter from regards to you and the poor man's good family.[26]

Another example of a privateer which was at least partly Manx owned was the *Enterprise*, in which George Moore junior held a part share. Between 1778 and 1781 she operated from Falmouth, intercepting French shipping, with some notable successes; the captured enemy vessels being turned over to the government in exchange for prize money. In February of 1779 it is reported that she was in Plymouth for repair following an encounter with a French frigate in which the latter came off second best. In July of that same year, she captured a Spaniard which was sent to Scotland. The *Enterprise* also recaptured the *Nancy Jenkins* out of Bristol bound for Antigua, which had been taken by the French, and brought her back to her home port. One of her crew around this time was John Errington Bacon, the eldest son of John Joseph Bacon. Through the influence of Moore, Bacon obtained the position of captain of marines on the *Enterprise*, at this time the Corps of Marines was expanding rapidly and parties of raw recruits were sometimes put aboard privateers to assist in boarding enemy vessels. Bacon's time on the ship was short lived however for it is recorded that he died at sea in 1780, possibly in a clash with an enemy warship, though no other details are available. The *Enterprise* continued to earn a steady revenue for her owners, all the more so when the refusal of Holland to end trade with the United States led Britain to declare war on the Dutch, who now became allies of the French. In December of that year young George Moore wrote that:

The war with Holland is likely to be continued with great rancour ... on both sides – the spirit of Privateering is very prevalent. The *Enterprise* had just returned to Falmouth having finished her Cruise but is already sailed on another and I hope will make up for lost time as the seas swarm with Dutch ships.[27]

With the Netherlands now in the war, in 1781 a squadron under Captain George Johnstone (once more at sea) was dispatched to the Cape of Good Hope, at that point one of Holland's overseas colonies, to seize it. The French naval bureau learned of the intention, and a French fleet sailed to protect the Dutch colony. An unexpected and inconclusive battle between the two forces took place in the Cape Verde islands, after which the French ships were able to reach the Cape first and reinforce the Dutch garrison. The squadron under Johnstone however continued south to the Cape, in the wake of the French, and upon arrival captured a number of Dutch East Indiamen sheltering in Saldanha Bay. The crews of the unprotected merchantmen were under orders to destroy their ships if the British appeared, but Johnstone was able to catch them unawares by flying French colours.

Interestingly one of Johnstone's vessels, HMS *Jupiter* under Captain Thomas Pasley, contained a number of Manxmen in its crew, and it is tempting to speculate that these were at least some of the unfortunates of the *Tyger* whom he had impressed two years earlier. Two of these men, William Lewin and Robert Colvin, were later able to report that a third Manxman on the *Jupiter*, Thomas Cretney of Santan, was ordered to form part of a prize crew which took over the captured Dutch East Indiaman *Dankbaarheid*. The prizes began their long journey back to Britain but the *Dankbaarheid*, a 1,000-ton ship armed with 24 guns, never arrived and was lost with all hands including Cretney, either to the weather or enemy action.

The year 1781 was also to be an auspicious one for one particular young sailor named William Bligh. It will be recalled that he had been aboard HMS *Ranger* in Douglas some time previously and in the intervening years had sailed with Captain James Cook, on his third and final voyage to the Pacific. Bligh had served as Master aboard HMS *Resolution*, commanded by Cook himself. The great explorer had made a deep impression upon Bligh both as a man of science and as an enlightened commander, and Bligh had been alongside him when he was killed by natives in Hawaii. It is interesting to note that on this expedition the ships had visited Australia, and Bligh had surveyed in more detail some of the areas first mapped by Furneaux and Peter Fannin.

Bligh had reached England once more in 1780, and then returned to the Isle of Man, where it seems that he spent about three months before his next appointment. With both Bligh and Fannin in Douglas at the same time, it seems unlikely that the two did not at least know of each other, and more than probable that they had met and discussed navigational matters. Bligh was then courting Elizabeth, the daughter of Richard Bethem, the first collector of customs on the Island after the Revestment, who lived at the Hague, Onchan. The couple were married at Onchan church in February 1781, but spent the first years of their married life in lodgings in Douglas. Shortly after his marriage, Bligh was appointed to serve in HMS *Belle Poule* as Master, and left for the war. Soon after he would fight in the Battle of Dogger Bank under Vice Admiral Sir Hyde Parker, before passing his lieutenant's examination. A letter written by Mrs Bligh from Douglas in July 1782 shows all the concern that a modern navy wife would have for a husband who had been posted on active service:

> I am not at present in the best Spirits, from the last accounts we received from England of the Combined Fleet and Ld. Howes being in great danger of meeting, however I trust in Providence and hope soon to hear that Mr. Bligh is safe returned to England – I shall write to him next week and hope he will be at Portsmouth to receive it.

In another letter later the same year she was equally concerned about her husband:

> I and my little Girl are well, but at present I am in a good deal of anxiety on Mr. Bligh's account as the last news we had from England was that sent home by Mr. Fitzherbert of Ld. Howes having relieved Giberalter [sic], which tho' it is looked upon, as it surely is, a piece of National success, yet must

leave those who have near connections in the Fleet in great anxiety as most probably the next news we may hear will be that there has been an engagement, however I do my best to keep up my Spirits, and trust that providence who has been so kind to me hitherto in preserving Mr Bligh will continue his goodness ... The last Newspaper I read made me very angry with Ld. Stewart for having refused to let Mr Bligh go with Capt. Pasley, as I see the *Jupiter* has been a very fortunate Ship.[28]

It seems that although it came to nothing, Pasley had perhaps offered Bligh a position aboard his ship, possibly the first evidence of contact between Bligh and the extended Heywood family.

During the early part of the American War the Royal Navy had mainly operated, rather unsuccessfully, in support of land operations against the colonists, and against Congress privateers. The entry of France into the conflict however brought a powerful enemy fleet into play. As well as assisting the Americans, the French hoped to eject the British from the West Indies. The British for their part began a campaign to eliminate French outposts and possessions in India. A number of British warships left Britain for Asian waters, in order to engage the French fleets there. Among these was HMS *Superb*, a 74-gun vessel. Many of the sailors on board were impressed, including John Cowl of Douglas, who wrote to his family, enclosing his will. The document also sheds much light on Cowl's fatalistic attitude, and love for his family, in what was to be his last letter:

On Board his Majesty Ship [sic] the *Superb* Lying at Spithead. Honoured Parents ... We intend to sail tomorrow without fail ... If I should not return home which Dr Brother I hope, youl keep [the property] for my sake and keep it in some sort of a Repair and Dispose of the rent as you think proper for my Dr Parents sake. I should never sell it which I hope youl keep it accordingly for your father and mother may have a place to put there [sic] Heads in their Old Days.

You wanted to know how I liked a man a war. Brother Its what I would Give all that I am worth to be Clear once more but now I am like to make the best of it this station. But I hope I shall have the Happiness To Drink a Pot of grog along with you once more. I shall never lose my heart Till I see Death before me. Dont forget you and my father to Drink my heath on Saturday night. So farewell, Dont forget my Mother.[29]

Cowl died at sea on the way to India, but another Manx sailor in the same fleet was Paul Lewin. He was aboard HMS *Hannibal* when she was captured by French ships off Sumatra in 1782. No words of Lewin's survive, but one of his shipmates named James Scurry, an ordinary seaman like Lewin, left a remarkable description of the capture of the *Hannibal* and the fate of her crew. After being taken aboard the French ships, many of the British sailors were routinely robbed. The conditions in which the captives were now to be held were less than humane; they were placed in the holds of the French ships and deprived of proper food and water, as sea battles continued to rage around them:

> We were on board their ships during two severe conflicts with our own fleet, commanded by Admiral Hughes. At those times we were all sent into the hold, but we should not have remained on deck, I presume, had we our choice. Many of us losing our clothes when taken, nothing remained to fill up the crevices of the cables on which our men slept; and I think, that stones would have been preferable to such a bed. From the commencement of each engagement, in some ships, the prisoners were not thought of till twenty-four hours after the termination of the affair; and all this time they were without water. In this situation were many, and the reader may easily judge of our condition; the hatches down, the natural heat of the

climate, the darkness and contractedness of the place, together with the smoke of the lower-deck guns descending through the gratings in columns, nearly suffocated several; and such was their extreme thirst, that several made use of their own water! But in this case the remedy was worse than the disease, for instead of allaying thirst, it excited it more strongly.[30]

Later he tells us how the unfortunate crew of the *Hannibal*, officers and men alike, were now sent ashore by the French commanders and handed over to France's long-term ally Hyder Ali, the sultan of the Kingdom of Mysore, in southern India. The British were supporters of Hyder Ali's rivals on the Indian subcontinent, the Marathas, so these prisoners were unlikely to be treated sympathetically:

At length we were all, to the number of 500, taken in the different ships by their fleet, landed, as before observed, at Cuddalore, after being on board their ships six months. The air and soil were witness to our joy at meeting; but alas! how transient! Our troubles, which we now supposed were drawing to a close, were just commencing! We were shortly escorted and sent to Chillembroom, one of Hyder Ali's strong forts. Here a dreadful famine raged; and our provisions consisted of bad rice and carrion beef; this, with the saltpetre ground on which we lay, was the cause of the loss of numbers of our men. I have seen many stout fellows taken one hour, and dead the next. Their disorder was the cramp, and, when seized, their distortions were such, that they scarcely retained the shape of human beings. What cause induced the French admiral to deliver us up to this unprincipled barbarian, we never could discover. We were equally at a loss to conceive, why we were abandoned by the English, when they might have demanded us. I can only attribute it to the deplorable state of British affairs in India during this period.[31]

THE AMERICAN WAR

Later the captured seamen were put in chains and marched through the jungle to another fortress prison, where bad food and disease were the order of the day. Many suffered ill treatment at the hands of Hyder Ali including forced conversion to Islam. It was in one of these prisons that Paul Lewin died.

Like a game of chess the two sides (later joined by the Spanish) moved their fleets between the Caribbean, the English Channel and the North American coast, hoping both to avoid destruction by hurricanes and at the same time achieve a tactical advantage. A Manx sailor aboard HMS *Shrewsbury,* Robert Colby, wrote home from Barbados to the mother of a dead shipmate in the Isle of Man in December 1781. He recounts the part that his ship had just played in one of the most important actions of the American Revolutionary War, the Battle of the Chesapeake, in September of that year. On this occasion a British force commanded by Rear Admiral Sir Thomas Graves met a French fleet led by Admiral François Joseph Paul, the Comte de Grasse. The battle was savage but inconclusive, though it represented a major strategic defeat for the British, since it prevented the Royal Navy from reinforcing or evacuating the blockaded forces of Lieutenant General Lord Cornwallis at Yorktown, Virginia.

In a two-hour engagement that took place after hours of manoeuvring, the lines of the two fleets did not completely meet, with only the forward and centre sections of the lines fully engaging. The two forces were consequently fairly evenly matched, although the British suffered more casualties and ship damage. The battle began with HMS *Intrepid* opening fire against the French ship *Marseillois*, its counterpart near the head of the line. The action very quickly became general, with the van and centre of each line fully engaged. The French tended to aim at British masts and rigging, with the intent of crippling their opponent's mobility. The effects of this tactic were apparent in the engagement: HMS *Shrewsbury* and HMS *Intrepid*, at the head of the British column, became virtually impossible to manage, and eventually fell out of the line. The battle broke off when the sun set. Colby gives a vivid description of the scene aboard the former ship, whilst his last sentence suggests that he was originally a merchant sailor in Manx waters:

> Alice Creech, this comes with my best respects to you, hoping these few lines will find you in good health as I am at present, thanks be to God for it. I am sorry to acquaint you of an engagement we had off Chesapeake Bay in America between the English and French fleet, our English fleet but consisting of nineteen ships of battle and the French fleet consisting of twenty-four ships of battle. We engaged each other for the space of two hours till our rigging was all shot away and sixty-four of our men killed and wounded. Out of them there was fourteen killed dead and several of the rest died of their wounds, one of which was your son John Creetch, of a wound he received in his breast and his right arm shot off. He died three days after the engagement and at that time he had two years pay due to him and some prize money, which would be of great service to you in your old days, if you could get some good friend to look after it for you.
>
> This ship's name is the *Shrewsbury*, mounting 74 guns, at present commanded by Captain John Knight but at that time it was captain Mark Robinson, where his leg was shot off and our first lieutenant killed. Please remember me to your daughters and to John Gordon and John Kelly living on the Bowling Green. So no more at present from Robert Colby who was servant at Mr Trugman's and sailed with Mr Lawson in the smack in Mr Tummans employ.[32]

De Grasse returned to the West Indies following the battle, harassing shipping and capturing British islands. His ultimate aim was to link up with Spanish forces and capture Jamaica, though in this he was to be thwarted by Admirals Rodney and Hood. A Manx sailor who was to lose his life in this campaign was Robert Cottier, one of the Cottiers of Narradale in Lezayre. He was also related to the Skillicorns and Caleys of that parish, and went to sea at an early age. In 1777 he had been a midshipman on the frigate HMS *Lowestoff*, at the same time that Lord Nelson was third lieutenant. At this time, she was under the command of Captain William Locker who can justifiably be regarded as one of Nelson's mentors. The future admiral was aged just 19, but his experiences with Locker and his teachings made a lasting impression upon him, and Nelson wrote fondly to him in later life expressing his gratitude. Cottier must have been a witness to this formative phase in Nelson's career, and perhaps he also received some seafaring knowledge from the future admiral. Cottier too must have found favour with Locker, for later that year he became Master's Mate on the *Lowestoff*. In 1780, he was appointed Master of that ship by Vice Admiral Sir Peter Parker. During this time the *Lowestoff* had been cruising in West Indian and American waters, and Cottier had taken part in the capture of several French West Indian islands as well as in the actions fought by Admiral Rodney off Martinique.

In February 1782, Cottier was appointed Master of the frigate HMS *Fox*, which was operating in the Caribbean in conjunction with HMS *Tickler*, a 12-gun brig-sloop. In the late nineteenth century Cottier's journal was still in the hands of his family, and though it is now lost some extracts survive. During the whole of the year 1782 nothing more important was referred to in this journal than the capture of a French brig. Early in 1783 however Cottier had an encounter with a French frigate. This is described in the last entry in his journal, for 24 January that year:

> Saw two strange sail to the southward. Set all sail to advantage; out all the reefs of the T sails; at 10 saw a strange sail in the N.E. Quarter. Made the *Tickler* signal to tack, which she answered. Fir'd a gun shotted at the Chase. The Chase hoisted French colours. Fir'd several guns shotted at the Chase as she was going in the harbour. Bore up and chas'd to the N.E.[33]

The ship's log however continues, and describes a battle the following day, in which Cottier was killed:

> About 1/4 past 11 being close up on the ship's quarter she hauled half up ... & began the action. We took in the fore topmast studded sail, hauled the Main sail up & bore up Parallel to her at less than half musquett shot Distance we in less than half an hour did not leave her a sail, yard or rope manageable. Her Fore Top mast with all its appurtenances was shot away and hung over her bow and she was in every respect a perfect wreck, notwithstanding which she made a second attempt to board us, but with as little success as the former, and to our very great astonishment considering her dismantled state & the great inequality of our crew, supported the action with extraordinary spirit for above half an hour upon when she was forced to surrender and proved the *Santa Catalina* Spanish Ship of war of only twenty two guns and 160 men.[34]

This was a classic small ship action. Although the large fleet battles are the ones remembered by history, it was through small frigates that naval power was actually applied, with captains working alone or almost alone, patrolling every day and engaging enemy vessels whenever they encountered them. The log of the *Fox* is silent about how Cottier's remains were disposed of, but a clue comes four days later when one of the wounded from the action died, and his body was committed to the deep.

Cottier was among the earliest of a new generation of Manx sailors who would make their career in the Royal Navy; the phenomenon became more apparent in the early 1780s as this trend continued to emerge among the seafarers of the Isle of Man. Whilst in the past participation in warfare in the Royal Navy had mostly been unwilling, with large numbers of Manxmen impressed, with the coming decade a new generation would begin to see life in the Royal Navy as a career option. There is no doubt that impressment was still resorted to, but increasingly we find examples of men like William Kelly, who volunteered to join the navy. He was born in Glen Dhoo in Ballaugh Parish in 1771, and his father was a minor land owner. The young William and his elder brother were among the boys who received their early education through the efforts of Bishop Hildesley, before spending some time at a school in Douglas. He entered the Royal Navy in 1781, aged just 10 years, according to his own statement of service going on board HMS *Nonsuch* as a landsman and later Able Seaman. To modern sensibilities this may seem a cruelly young age for a boy to be going aboard a warship, but it was by no means uncommon in this era. With so much to learn about how to handle a ship and its crew, it was essential that these young gentlemen started early; often they were employed as officer's servants or messengers. The ship was under the command of Captain William Truscott; the *Nonsuch* was then in the West Indies, and Kelly must have been present at Admiral Rodney's defeat and capture of his enemy de Grasse on 12 April 1782.

In December of that year 1782 the sloop HMS *Echo*, recently built at Liverpool and about to undertake service on the Newfoundland station, began recruiting on the Isle of Man. More than twenty Manx sailors were enlisted by one of her officers, Lieutenant Hodson, and almost all were volunteers. The testimony of two of the men survives in the Chancery Court records of the Isle of Man. One of them, William Moore petitioned to be released from Castle Rushen (where he was he was being held for non-payment of money owed to a woman who had affiliated him as the father of her child) in order to proceed on service with the *Echo*. The other, Francis John Dessau, stated that he had voluntarily enlisted in order to escape his debts, and petitioned likewise to be allowed to proceed to Liverpool. He was successful, because the Royal Navy would protect those who owed £20 or less from their creditors. Interestingly the books record him as born at Dunkirk. Of the twenty Manxmen enlisted, only one deserted in Liverpool. The acting captain of the *Echo*, before she left the Mersey for North American waters, was Robert Parry Young, and his son Robert Benjamin Young was also aboard for a short time.

Popular support for the American war began to wane in Britain after the defeat at Yorktown, and in April 1782 the House of Commons voted to end hostilities. Preliminary peace treaties were signed with America and her allies in November of that year, though it would be a further twelve months before the Treaty of Paris and the Treaty of Versailles formally ended the conflict. Hugh Crow was by now on a return journey from the West Indies, with the ship laden with sugar bound for London. Many of the crew had deserted, including the carpenter, so Crow, who had a knowledge of boat building from his boyhood in Ramsey, filled the void. By now, the press gang was no longer a threat. He continues:

> Towards the latter end of our voyage our provisions and water began to get short, but our minds were relieved by our safe arrival in the Downs in January, 1783. We had let go our anchor and were furling the sails, when we heard the pilot joyfully shout that England was at peace with all the world. The delight which this intelligence diffused amongst us was extreme, although we were, at the time, suffering severely both from cold and hunger. On our arrival in London I lamented to observe the abandoned and profligate conduct of the sailors in that vast metropolis; for government was then paying off the crews of the men-of-war, and many of those ill-starred thoughtless beings, after squandering their hard-earned gains with reckless and wasteful precipitancy, were reduced almost to a state of beggary and starvation.[35]

Eight months after the end of the war, on 5 July 1783, a Manx sailor named Thomas Carroll wrote to his mother from Chatham where his ship HMS *Alfred* was in the process of discharging her crew:

> Dear mother i take this Opportunity to write you these few lines and Hoping that they will find you in Good Health as I am att Present thank God for it and to Lett you Now that

THE AMERICAN WAR

> i shall be att Home in about 3 weeks as we are Clearing our Ship as fast as possible as My Brother is dead if he as left any will and Power with you for you to send it to me and i will do what i can for to gett His wages and Prizes Money for you and if Not for you to Get the Power of aturney for to Get it and send it to me by the Return of the Post or i shall Not Have time to Get it Before i am Paid of from the Ship i take it very unkind that [you] could not send me an answer to Any of my leters this four years Remember me to my Brothers Sisters and let them No that i shall be att Home soon ...[36]

Carroll's brother had died in the West Indies where he had also served, indeed it is possible that they were shipmates. The war would cast a shadow not just across those families like his who had lost a son. For other humble Manx families the cost would be financial, as they could be reduced to beggary if a breadwinner had been badly injured or maimed. One ex-sailor, Anthony Kermeen of Malew wrote:

> ...during the American War [I] served for the term of 6 years on board of one of his Majesty's Ships ... in a certain engagement [I] incurred the misfortune of a severe wound in [the] leg & in consequence thereof was discharged but unfortunately allowed no pension. Yet the wound received being never effectually cured sometimes so affects [me I am] rendered incapable of pursuing [my] daily labours yet the little money which [I] acquire when in a tolerable capacity of doing so is generally expended on medical assistance for [my] leg.[37]

Peace however also led to the scaling down of the Royal Navy, which meant that many officers and others who had wished to make it their career had no option but to leave the service, at least for a spell. Both William Kelly and William Bligh left the Royal Navy at this time. We do not know precisely how Kelly earned a living in the following years but he was more than likely at sea in a civilian capacity. Likewise in the mid-1780s Bligh became an officer in the merchant service, sailing aboard vessels owned by his wife's uncle Duncan Campbell. In order to do this Bligh required the consent of the navy, and in July 1783 he wrote from his home in Douglas to Campbell to inform him that the necessary permission had been granted. The letter also sheds an interesting sidelight on Bligh's domestic arrangements at this time, and on commercial life in Douglas in general, for he adds:

> Mrs Bligh and I have begun housekeeping and find it a most agreeable change from lodgings. We have one of the neater houses in Town for eight guineas a year and have with little trouble furnished it very decently. The season of the year too is very plentiful and all kinds of provisions very cheap. The only disadvantage that people labour under here [is] that those who buy have scarce any just weight or measure for notwithstanding here are proper magistrates, they never interfere ... The Herring fishery on which most of the inhabitants depend and is the only thing by which money immediately circulates through the Island, is not yet begun, there being no show of fish and it is feared it will turn out a very scarce season, this will mishap the people much as it is the only work they go about with alacrity or reap equal benefit.[38]

The Blighs at this time worshipped at Old St Matthew's, on the harbourside, where their second daughter Mary was baptised in 1784. This probably indicates that they were living within sight of the harbour. Fletcher Christian, his brother Humphrey, and his sister Mary together with their mother Ann, in exile from debt incurred in England, all lived at this time on Fort Street, a mere stone's throw from St Matthew's. Although Fletcher Christian was born in Cumberland, his father had died young, and left his mother in financial difficulties. By the early 1780s she and her younger children were living in Douglas. Fletcher Christian remained at Cockermouth Grammar School until he was 16, and for the next two years he lived with his mother, brother and sister. Fletcher's branch of the family (the Christians of Ewanrigg) was an offshoot of the Manx Christian family, and he was a descendant on his father's side of William Christian (Illiam Dhone). Furthermore, he owed his unusual first name to the fact that he was descended on his mother's side from the Fletchers, who in the Isle of Man had lived at Ballafletcher. Like many notable families in the eighteenth century, the Fletchers and the Christians had both a Cumberland and a Manx branch, and in this era the links between the two regions were much stronger. In the days of Derby rule, Liverpool had been the chief port for the Isle of Man, but under the Atholls this had moved to Whitehaven, before reverting back to Liverpool in modern times.

Fletcher Christian was 19 years old when he made his first sea voyage as a crewman, which was late in life by the standards of the day. He seems to have opted for a career at sea almost as a last resort, after the family's funds ran out. He was not able to attend university as his older brothers Charles (who studied medicine at Edinburgh) and Edward (who read law and later became a senior judge) had done. Yet he took quickly to life at sea. In 1783 he had been on the books of HMS *Eurydice* outward bound for a twenty-one month voyage to India. The ship's muster shows Christian's conduct was more than satisfactory because some seven months out from England, he had been promoted from Midshipman to Master's Mate. Later, his brother Charles wrote of this journey:

> I met with a surgeon in East India who had gone out with him in the *Eurydice* Frigate, commanded by the Honourable Captain Courtney, and also with an officer on my return to London who had sailed in the same ship with Fletcher. They corroborated to me his Assertions – Captain Courtney had appointed him to act as Lieutenant. They said he was strict, yet as it were played while he wrought with the men – he made a Toil a pleasure and ruled over them in a pleasant manner superior to any young officer they had seen.[39]

From this we gain a picture of a confident well-bred young man, at ease with commanding others of a lower social status, but not necessarily aloof from them. After this, he undertook two trading voyages with William Bligh to Jamaica, on ships belonging to Duncan Campbell. Christian had almost certainly been introduced to Bligh by John Taubman, and one document states that:

> It cannot be reconciled with Christian's [later] conduct that Major Taubman, of the Nunnery, in the Isle of Man, can testify, viz, that from his recommendation of Captain Bligh as a navigator, Christian voluntarily preferred sailing with Captain Bligh as a common man in a West India ship, till there was a vacancy among the officers, to the immediate appointment to the rank of mate in another ship.[40]

Bligh it seems was at first reluctant to take him, replying politely that he already had his full compliment of officers, but Christian now wrote directly to him, telling him that he would go as an ordinary seaman, in order to gain experience:

> ... Wages are no object; [I] only wish to learn my profession, and if [you] would permit me to mess with the gentlemen, [I] would readily enter your ship as a Foremastman, until there was a vacancy among the officers ... We Midshipmen are gentlemen, we never pull at a rope; I should even be glad to go on one voyage in that situation, for there may be occasions, when officers may be called upon to do the duties of a common man.[41]

The stage was thus set for one of the greatest naval dramas in history to unfold.

* * *

THE AMERICAN WAR

The twenty or so years since the Revesting Act had seen almost no investment in the Isle of Man. The British government, having assumed the sovereignty of the Island, had taken no steps whatsoever in that time to promote the prosperity of the place or its people. The official attitude during those years seems to have been that the Island was a viper's nest of smugglers, and most of the time thought was only given to what could be extracted from it in terms of revenue, rather than what should be ploughed back in from what was raised there in customs. The Island's harbours in particular were in dire need of improvement and nothing illustrated this better than an incident which occurred at this time. Peter Fannin as a note to the plan of Douglas tells us that on:

> Sunday, 19th November 1786, Douglas Lighthouse and 82 yards of the quay was washed down in a gale of easterly wind.[42]

Yet a further disaster, even more terrible, occurred the following year as a direct result. David Robertson, the author of *A Tour through the Isle of Man*, appears to have been an eyewitness to this tragic event:

> The entrance of the harbour is narrow and dangerous, being fenced on each side by a range of precipices. In the centre of these, a lighthouse, at once useful and ornamental, formerly stood. This, with a great part of the quay, was destroyed by a severe storm in 1786; and in this ruinous state, highly injurious to the public, and fatal to many individuals, it has remained ever since. To enumerate the various shipwrecks this neglect has occasioned would be unnecessary; but the awful calamity which happened in September 1787 is too interesting to be passed over in silence ... The herring ground was then off Clay-head and Laxey, about three leagues from Douglas. In the evening when the boats again sailed thither, there were no indications of a change in the weather; but at midnight a brisk

equinoctial gale arose, and the fishermen, impelled by their usual timidity, fled to the harbour of Douglas for refuge.

On the ruins of the lighthouse is fixed a slender post, from which is hung a small lantern. This wretched substitute was thrown down by one of the first boats in its eagerness to gain the harbour. The consequences were dreadful. In a few minutes all was horror and confusion. The darkness of the night, the raging of the sea, the vessels dashing against the rocks, the cries of the fishermen perishing in the waves, and the shrieks of the women ashore, imparted such a sensation of horror, as none but a spectator can possibly conceive. When the morning came it presented an awful spectacle; the beach and rocks covered with wrecks, and a group of dead bodies floating in the harbour. In some boats whole families perished. The shore was crowded with women, some in all the frantic agony of grief, alternately weeping over the corpses of father, brother, and husband.[43]

Evidence of the loss of the Herring Fleet can be found in many parish registers from this era, with groups of young men, sometimes from the same family, buried together.

Only by the mid-1780s, with the American war over, did the Isle of Man slowly begin to return to some form of prosperity. There were still strong trading links between the Island and the West Indies, as well as with European ports. Some important and powerful families made up the social elite, and again their links and influence spread beyond the shores of the Isle of Man. There was some association with the army, but it was with the Royal Navy that Manx influence and involvement would increase in the next twenty or so years.

Chapter 3

The Pacific and the Far East

The loss of the American colonies encouraged Britain to look to the east, and expansion into the Pacific continued apace since Cook had first charted Australia. In India, Britain faced rival Dutch and French forces, as well as hostility from native rulers. In this brief period of peace, Britain also made her first contact with imperial China. However one story from the late eighteenth century above all others has simultaneously captured the imagination both of serious naval historians, and of the public at large. It is that of the mutiny aboard HMS *Bounty*, led by Fletcher Christian against the captain, Lieutenant William Bligh.

There are many unanswered questions surrounding the mutiny and its aftermath. The fact that the story has its origins in the Isle of Man has, however, largely escaped the attention of all but the most dedicated scholars. Yet three of the main protagonists had associations with the Island, and Douglas could with justification be said to be the birthplace of the mutiny. Certainly William Bligh was quick to assert the Manx character of the plot against him in his first correspondence regarding the incident subsequently.

Although the closure of the American War had brought with it some measure of peace, it also entailed the loss of the continental United States as a source of cheap food for the slaves on the British plantations in the West Indies. These plantations, and the sugar which they produced, were a major pillar of the British economy at this time, indeed sugar was worth four times the value of tobacco which had been the major export of the lost American colonies. Tax on sugar was of vital importance to the exchequer, thus the planters of the West Indies with their revenue potential carried a great deal of political weight. The slave trade, as we have seen, was inextricably bound up with all aspects of commerce in Britain at this time.

A new source of food was needed for the slaves, and the eminent botanist Sir Joseph Banks proposed that that Breadfruit, with its large edible seedpods, might provide the answer. He suggested that seedlings could be transported from their native habitat in Tahiti, in the Pacific, and might successfully then be grown in the West Indies. Such was the leverage exercised by the plantation owners that they were able to put pressure on the Admiralty to provide a vessel and crew for an expedition to acquire a supply of these plants. Even so, the Royal Navy did not feel that it was appropriate to send one of its warships for this purpose, and thus a vessel was taken up from trade. The merchantman *Bethia* was purchased, armed, fitted out to transport the precious plants, and renamed HMS *Bounty*. Banks wanted an able navigator who knew the waters both of the South Pacific and the Caribbean to command her, and in this respect, William Bligh was a natural choice. Bligh had sailed with Cook, and had proved himself a capable navigator in the Pacific. His journeys to Jamaica as a merchant captain meant that he knew those waters equally well. Bligh was ambitious and eager for promotion. In the peace time navy this could be slow, and so he was anxious to be assigned to the mission, in the hope of making a name for himself.

The Manx links to the *Bounty* expedition are strong, indeed it could be argued that whilst the mission was conceived in London, Douglas was the cradle of the personal relationships which would spark the most famous mutiny in British history. Furthermore the claim could also be made that most *Bounty* scholars have failed fully to understand the close network of Manx political and social relationships which were at work here. William Bligh, the young naval lieutenant who lived in the Isle of Man in the 1780s, already had a natural choice for the position of Master's Mate in Fletcher Christian, with whom he had sailed twice already on his voyages to Jamaica, and in whose social circles he moved, but the relationship goes deeper than this. After Christian's widowed mother Ann had fled to the

Isle of Man in 1779 to escape her debts in England, she and her family came under the patronage of the most powerful member of the Christian clan, John Christian (later in life known as John Christian Curwen) who held Milntown and Unerigg, and was to be both a member of the House of Keys and a member of Parliament. The Christian family had arranged for Ann and her children, Fletcher, his sister Mary and his brother Humphrey, to live on a stipend in genteel poverty in a house on Fort Street in Douglas, a matter of a few hundred yards from where Lieutenant and Mrs Bligh lived after their marriage. Their de facto guardian at this time must have been John Taubman. Bligh of course also knew the Taubman family, so there is a strong probability that John Taubman introduced him to Fletcher Christian.

If St Matthew's was the likely cradle for the Bligh-Christian relationship, then St George's seems to have performed the same role in the Bligh-Heywood association. St Matthew's was regarded at this time as the 'Manx' church, and many of the social elite of the town worshipped instead at St George's, the 'English' church. It seems likely that here the contacts were made which led to Peter Heywood's part in the Mutiny on the *Bounty*. The Taubman family, who resided at the Nunnery, the Heywoods who had returned to Douglas, and the Bethems were almost certainly in this congregation around the same time.

As a favour for his father-in-law Richard Bethem, Bligh took on board as an honorary Midshipman 16-year-old Peter Heywood, whose family lived at The Parade, again a matter of just a few hundred yards from both the Blighs and Christians. The boy had recently left St Bees School where he had received a typical gentleman's education involving instruction in the classics and Latin. He had already completed a year in the Royal Navy, albeit in the shore-bound HMS *Powerful* at Plymouth. Although the Heywoods had important contacts in the navy, not least in the form of Peter's uncle Captain Thomas Pasley, the family at this time was in financial difficulty; Peter John Heywood had been dismissed by the Duke of Atholl for mismanagement and embezzlement of funds. Pasley for his part was under no illusion about the male members of the Heywood family, writing to John Taubman in February 1787:

> All my connections on your side of the water I have but a very bad opinion of, and I speak from unerring experience ... as to Peter [John] he really has good sense ... That desires not common sense For I think I may be bold to say that he never did any sensible action in his life – so much for my Relations.[44]

William Bligh's father-in-law Richard Bethem was anxious to try to assist the family by advancing Peter Heywood's naval career. In September 1787 he wrote from Douglas to Bligh, then in London, to recommend Peter to him:

> He is an ingenious young lad & has always been a favourite of mine & indeed every body here ... And indeed the Reason of my insisting so strenuously upon his going the Voyage with you is that after I had mentioned the matter to Mrs Bligh, his Family have fallen into a great deal of Distress on account of their Father's losing the Duke of Atholl's business, and I thought it would not appear well in me to drop this matter if it cou'd be possibly be done without any prejudice to you, as this wou'd seem deserting them in their adversity, and I found they wou'd regard it as a great Disappointment ... I hope he will be of some Service to you, so far as he is able, in writing or looking after any necessary matters under your charge...[45]

For his part, Bligh was happy to oblige thus offering Heywood his first experience of life at sea, and his first rung on the naval promotion ladder. The two official positions for Midshipmen had been assigned to men under the patronage of Sir Joseph Banks, so Bligh took Heywood on board as an Able Seaman on the ship's books, a common practice at the time, though such 'young gentlemen' lived and messed with the officers rather than the men. Immediately before the voyage, Fletcher met in London with his older brother Charles Christian, a ship's surgeon with the Honourable

THE PACIFIC AND THE FAR EAST

East India Company who had just returned from the east. There had been a mutiny aboard his vessel, and some have speculated that it was news of this incident which sparked Fletcher's later actions. Charles Christian was afterwards anxious to refute this suggestion, and has left a fascinating account of his final meeting with his brother, and the mood in which he found him:

> When the *Middlesex* returned from India, the *Bounty* lay near to where she was moored. Fletcher came on Board coming up the River, and he and I and one of our officers who had been in the Navy went on Shore, and spent the evening and remained till next Day; he was then full of professional Ambition and of Hope. He bared his Arm, and I was amazed at its Brawniness. 'This', says he, 'has been acquired by hard labour.' He said, 'I delight to set the men an Example. I not only can do every part of a common sailor's Duty, but am on a par with the principal part of the Officers.'[46]

With regard to the *Bounty* herself, there were a number of problems in using a ship of this nature for this purpose; she was too small to begin with. Secondly and for reasons perhaps connected with this, when she sailed she carried no marines, always essential for the maintenance of discipline aboard a warship. Bligh's orders had been to take the shorter route to the Pacific around Cape Horn, but she arrived too late in the year and the weather was too bad for her to accomplish this.

Bligh's decision to turn east and take the longer route around the Cape of Good Hope was, Heywood records, to the great joy of everyone on board. Yet tensions and divisions were already apparent. Bligh was dissatisfied with the Master, John Fryer's handling of the ship, and appointed Fletcher Christian as Acting Lieutenant above him. Whilst the decision can only have been perceived by Fryer as an insult, it also demonstrates the high regard for Christian which Bligh held at this point in the mission. At the same time, a strong bond seems to have developed between Christian and Peter Heywood. As well as the common domestic link which the two shared, they were also distantly related by marriage. More than this however they shared the experience of being born into wealth and privilege but having the humiliation of losing almost everything except their family name. During the voyage, Christian took Heywood under his wing and taught him navigation.

After a long and arduous journey, the *Bounty* reached Tahiti, with which Bligh was familiar from his voyage with Cook. The Breadfruit seedlings would take several months to germinate and grow into plants strong enough to be transported, but Bligh, instead of taking his ship on a further mapping expedition of the Pacific, allowed his men the time to recuperate and rest. Here they fell into Tahitian ways. The Island was the subject of many a sailor's yarn, for its women were both beautiful and by European standards uninhibited. Many of the *Bounty*'s crew formed relationships with the enchanting Tahitian women, and it has been argued that here the bonds of discipline began to unravel. Both Fletcher Christian and Peter Heywood were treated by the ship's surgeon for venereal disease whilst at Tahiti – immediately before arrival, Bligh had ordered every man on the *Bounty* to be inspected for the disease by the surgeon and he records that all had been reported to be free of it. The tropical paradise of Tahiti must have seemed like a long way from Douglas, and not only in terms of distance and weather.

Upon the return journey, Bligh attempted to re-impose some of the discipline which had been lost. Fletcher Christian was the subject of some of his verbal dressings down, often in front of the crew, and one particular incident – trivial in retrospect – involved coconuts found to be missing from a barrel on deck. Bligh called Christian a thief, a direct and personal insult. Shortly after leaving Tahiti, in April 1789, the Acting Lieutenant Fletcher Christian led part of the crew in a mutiny against Bligh. The mutineers, having seized the arms chest, dragged Bligh and his loyal crew on deck. After Christian had seized the ship, a heated exchange took place between him and the captain. Peter Heywood later described what he saw that day:

When I awoke & laying my cheek upon the side of my hammock chanced to look into the main Hatchway where I saw Matthew Thompson seaman, sitting upon an arm chest which was there secured with a drawn cutlass in his Hand; and as I knew him to be a man who had kept the middle watch with Mr Wm Peckover the gunner, I was struck with surprise at a sight so unusual; unable to conjecture the reason of his being there at so early an hour, I immediately got out of bed, went to the side of the birth [sic], and asked him what he was doing there? Upon which he replied 'That Mr Fletcher Christian, who had the watch upon deck, had taken the ship from the Captain, whom he had confined upon deck, & was going to carry him home as a prisoner & that they should have more provisions and better usage than before.'

W. Elphinstone one of the master's mates, who was then lying awake in his hammock, which hung at the outside of the opposite birth [sic] likewise heard what this man said to me. I immediately dressed myself & went up the fore Hatchway upon deck & having got upon the Booms on the Larboard side, I went aft as far as the Quarter of the boats, I saw the Captain standing on the Larboard side of the Quarter deck, a little before the Bittacle, in his shirt, with his hands tied behind his back, & Mr Christian standing on the right hand side of him with a drawn bayonet in his hand and a small pocket pistol in his pocket; he was giving orders to Mr Cole the Boatswain (who was upon deck) to hoist the large cutter out, the small one having been got out some time before; upon this I came a little farther forward & went over to the other side, I saw Mr Christian beckon to Mr Thomas Hayward (who with Mr John Hallet was standing on the Quarter deck, between the two four pounders) he said to him, 'get yourself ready to go in the boat, sir' – and Mr Hayward made answer 'Why? Mr Christian what harm did I ever do you that you should be so hard upon me; I hope you won't insist upon it' but he again repeated the same order to him & to Mr John Hallet who seemed to be in tears & answered 'I hope not sir' – hearing this, & being afraid that if I was in his sight he might give me the same orders, which I feared very much.[47]

Heywood was told that the plan was to put Bligh and his fellow officers in the boat, and land them on the nearby island of Tofua, which he knew to be inhabited by particularly savage warriors. Faced with a choice as he saw it between death by natives or from starvation, he hoped to be able to remain upon the *Bounty*. Confiding his thoughts in fellow midshipman Thomas Hayward, he received a scornful reply to the effect that Hayward wished that he had a choice, but that Christian had ordered him into the boat. This was probably the cause of Hayward's harsh attitude towards Heywood when the two met again later. The latter continued:

> I assured myself ... that in our present situation my intentions therefore to remain in the ship were not improper & I was confirmed in this opinion by Mr Bligh telling several of the men (when he was in the launch) who were endeavouring to get into the Boat, 'for God's sake my lads don't any more of you come into the boat I'll do you justice if ever I should get home.' Thus he prevented them and they remained in the ship.[48]

Heywood was later confined below in his cabin by the mutineers, and thus had no further opportunity of joining Bligh in the launch. Much has been written about this incident; it was almost unheard of for a crew to mutiny on the return leg of a journey, and Bligh's cruelty towards his crew cited as a factor in the uprising; in fact statistically he flogged his men less than many other captains. Seamen accepted the harsh discipline of life at sea stoically. If they were at fault, they expected to be punished. What roused their ire was injustice, and Bligh was a man of temper who was prone to erratic outbursts. So much for the disaffection of the crew, but what could have caused such a dramatic fracture in the personal relationship between Bligh and Christian? Charles Christian for his part later referred to a conversation which took place perhaps on the Isle of Man, and placed the blame upon Bligh's meanness of spirit, which had goaded his brother beyond restraint:

> When Major Taubman asked Bligh what could possibly be the cause of his Defection, he replied it was Insanity. He spoke right. But who was it that had drove him into that unhappy state? Fletcher when a boy was slow to be moved [but] jealousy and tyranny had produced ill-usage to so great an excess as to fix his soul ... and Revenge ensued as an effervescence from the opposition of good to bad qualities. What scurrilous abuse! What provoking insult to one of the chief officers on Board for having taken a Cocoa Nut from a heap to quench his thirst when on Watch – base, mean-minded wretch![49]

As for Heywood, it seems that he saw himself as merely an innocent bystander in the affair, and along with other Bligh loyalists who could not be accommodated in the launch, he asked to remain on the *Bounty* and to be put ashore at Tahiti to await the next Royal Navy vessel. What Heywood, who was after all only 16, had perhaps not appreciated, is that the Royal Navy does not recognise neutrality in a mutiny situation. There can be no standing on the sidelines, and those who do not do all in their power to try to suppress a mutiny are deemed also to be guilty of the crime.

After Bligh and some of his crew were placed in the ship's launch an incredible journey of over over 1,000 miles took them to Timor in the Dutch East Indies. He at once took the opportunity of writing to his wife, and this letter dated 19 August 1789 has become famous in *Bounty* folklore:

> On the 28th. April at day light in the morning Christian having the morning watch, He with several others came into

my Cabbin while I was a Sleep, and seizing me, holding naked Bayonets at my Breast, tied my Hands behind my back, and threatened instant distruction if I uttered a word. I however call'd loudly for assistance, but the conspiracy was so well laid that the Officers Cabbin Doors were guarded by Centinels, so that Nelson, Peckover, Samuels [ie Samuel] or the Master could not come to me. I was now dragged on Deck in my Shirt & closely guarded – I demanded of Christian the cause of such a violent act, & severely degraded him for his Villainy but he could only answer – 'not a word Sir or you are Dead.' I dared him to the act & endeavored to rally some one to a sense of their duty but to no effect. Besides this Villain see young Heywood one of the ringleaders, & besides him see Stewart joined with him. Christian I had assured of promotion when he came home, & with the other two I was every day rendering them some service – It is incredible! these very young Men I placed every confidence in, yet these great Villains joined with the most able Men in the Ship got possession of the Arms and took the *Bounty* from me, with huzza's for Otaheite. I have now reason to curse the day I ever knew a Christian or a Heywood or indeed a Manks man.[50]

The interesting point about this letter, which many *Bounty* scholars seem to have overlooked, is that Bligh immediately saw the mutiny as Manx in origins, and believed that it must in some way have been cooked up by Christian and Heywood together, simply because they originated from Douglas and were on close terms personally, when it should have been obvious that the latter had had at best a minor part in at, and that many of the true ringleaders had no connection to the Isle of Man.

When Bligh returned home, he was perceived as nothing short of a hero. His incredible journey in an open boat with meagre rations and only his navigational skills to fall back upon remains an outstanding feat to this day, rarely equalled, let alone surpassed, in the more than 200 years which have followed. The controversy surrounding Bligh's command of the *Bounty*, and the anti-hero status accorded to Christian in various Hollywood productions, lay yet in the future. For the moment, those in Bligh and Christian's social circle were aghast at what had happened, but the two sides were already forming up against one another. As well as Major John Taubman, Bligh met with Fletcher's brother Edward, and with his cousin John Christian Curwen to put his side of events. Fletcher's other brother Charles meanwhile wrote of his expectation of an explanation for his actions. He thought that:

> It would be found that there had been some Cause not then known that had driven Fletcher to this desperate Step ... when Men are cooped up for a long Time in the Interior of a Ship, there oft prevails such jarring Discordancy of Tempers and Conduct that it is enough on many Occasions by repeated Acts of Irritation and Offence to change the Disposition of a Lamb to that of an Animal fierce and resentful. What can not the Power of Provocation bring to pass on land, where there is free range for separation?[51]

Charles Christian for his part also felt keenly the implication that it must have been he who had planted the idea of mutiny in his brother's head, following the uprising on the *Middlesex*, writing of how he came across:

> ... the heart-rending account of the *Bounty's* mutiny. I was struck with Horror, and weighed down with sorrow to so extreme a pitch that I became stupefied. It was hard to bear, but I thank God, strength was given to me equal to the Burthen. I knew that this unfortunate occurrence following so close upon the heels of my late eventful and disastrous voyage would occasion the lies which had been spread abroad in consequence to assume the aspect of truth.[52]

Meanwhile, another Royal Navy vessel, HMS *Pandora* had been dispatched to the Pacific to search for the mutineers. Fletcher Christian parted company with Peter Heywood at Tahiti, the latter choosing to remain and wait for another Royal Navy ship, the former heading on to find Pitcairn Island, wrongly positioned on British charts, where he and the other mutineers, together with some Tahitian men and women would form a colony.

Heywood meanwhile spent his time learning the language of the people and compiling an Anglo-Tahitian dictionary. When the *Pandora* finally reached Tahiti on 23 March 1791 Heywood took a canoe and rowed out through the surf to meet her. Deeply tanned, wearing a grass skirt and with a number of tattoos, he must have offered an unorthodox impression of a British naval officer, and Heywood was received coolly by the crew of the *Pandora;* in particular he was treated with disdain by another former member of the *Bounty* crew, Midshipman (now Lieutenant) Thomas Hayward. The Captain of the *Pandora*, Edward Edwards ordered an eleven by eighteen foot cage to be constructed on deck (nicknamed 'Pandora's Box') into which all the *Bounty* men at Tahiti were thrown for the duration of the journey back to England, where they were all to face trial for mutiny. Heywood wrote to his mother:

> We were all put in close confinement with both legs and both hands in irons & were treated with great rigour, not being allowed to ever get out of this place & being obliged to eat drink sleep & obey the calls of nature here you may form some idea of the disagreeable situation I must have been in (unable to help myself, being deprived of the use of both my legs and hands) but by no means adequate to the reality – such as I am unable to represent.[53]

The *Pandora* set sail for the Friendly Islands, in search of the *Bounty* but found no trace. From here they sailed westward, but the *Pandora* ran aground as she attempted to return through the Great Barrier Reef, off the eastern coast of Australia, on 29 August 1791. Heywood was lucky to survive, being released from his irons only at the last minute. The journey home continued in open boats, before transfer to HMS *Gorgon*. When he reached Britain at last, he was put on trial for his life. It was said that his sister Nessy, upon hearing the news, left the Isle of Man immediately in the dead of night, by means of a fishing boat. Her attempts to cajole, persuade and implore those in positions of authority ultimately led to his pardon. The efforts of his uncle Thomas Pasley also undoubtedly had much to do with this, leading to mutterings in some quarters that those with influence had saved their necks, whilst those without had gone to the gallows.

Fletcher Christian's other brother Humphrey also went to sea, and became the mate aboard a slave ship. He died at Bonny on the coast of West Africa in 1790, when his vessel exploded. This was not an uncommon occurrence, as gunpowder was one of the staple commodities traded in Africa for slaves. He was clearly one of the leading figures of young Douglas society in the years prior to his death, and moved in the same circles as his contemporary the satirical poet John Stowell, who published under the *nom de plume* 'Tom the Gardener'. Stowell wrote an ode to Humphrey Christian, upon his death. He also wrote one for Nessy Heywood, also part of his social circle, and thus Stowell provides another link between the Heywood and Christian families. Yet the fact that Humphrey Christian met his end in the fashion he did is telling indeed as to how far the fortunes of his branch of the family had fallen. Hugh Crow in describing the crews of slave ships referred to them as wretched beings, often fleeing from crimes or creditors, and stated that aboard his ships:

> I have known many gentleman's sons of desperate character and abandoned habits, who had either for some offence, or had involved themselves in pecuniary embarrassments, as to have become outcasts unable to procure the necessaries of life.[54]

It was a phrase which could almost have referred directly to Humphrey Christian, or indeed to his brother Fletcher. Hugh Crow for his part was in Jamaica at the time Humphrey died, aboard a merchant ship called the *Elizabeth*, and shortly returned with her to Liverpool. In doing so he again encountered the hated press gang, which he regarded as an evil greater even than the slave trade:

> When about making the land near Cape Clear, we learned from a brig of war that England was on the eve of going to war with Spain: we were therefore apprehensive of being impressed. We came to anchor at the N.W. buoy early in August, 1790, after a short passage; and there, in the greatest hurry and confusion we took to the boats to avoid those land-sharks, the pressgang. Some of the men having got half drunk we were as nearly drowned as possible, by running aground on a bank on the Formby side, in the night. There were at the time several tenders in the river, with their holds crammed full of poor impressed sailors and landsmen. These press rooms were little better than pigsties: yet hardly a word was said, or a murmur raised, by our great statesmen, about the pitiable condition of those who crowded these receptacles of misery. All the talk, all the commiseration of the day, was about the black slaves: the white slaves were thought unworthy of consideration, although I cannot help thinking that the charity of those who held such 'palaver' ought in justice to have begun at home. On this occasion we had the good fortune to escape the pressgang, and I once more found myself safe and sound in Liverpool.[55]

The incident which Crow describes was the Nootka Crisis of 1790, in which a dispute over trading rights in western Canada led to the so-called Spanish Armament. War with Spain appeared likely, and the Royal Navy began to mobilise its manpower by impressing sailors and landsmen alike. Many half-pay retired officers were also recalled to the service, including Lieutenant Henry Inman, a 28-year-old who had seen a good deal of action in the American Revolutionary War. Inman was initially posted to a ship of the line, but when the looming crisis with Spain blew over, he was sent instead to the Isle of Man, which seems to have been a pleasant enough station for a young naval officer in peacetime. The *Naval Chronicle* tells us much about Lieutenant Inman's posting to Douglas in 1791, in command of a naval vessel based in the harbour. In the article, which was probably penned by Inman himself, he refers to himself in the third person, as was fashionable at the time:

> ... he was removed to the command of the *Pigmy* cutter, of 14 guns, stationed at the Isle of Man. To a young officer of spirit, such an appointment is very desirable and satisfactory: desirable, as it affords opportunities for the display of gallantry, not always to be obtained, on account of rank, in larger ships; satisfactory as proving that zeal and abilities are not, at all times, unnoticed. The *Pigmy* was not of the largest class of cutters, nor a very prime sailer: and though her commander was not fortunate in his captures in consequence, perhaps, of the latter circumstance a combination of events rendered the command, and the station on which she was employed, delightful. At this period, Lieutenant Inman formed a matrimonial alliance with Miss Dalby, the sister of Captain Dalby, of the royal navy. The civility and politeness which every officer on the Isle of Man station is sure to experience from the inhabitants, are almost proverbial. To Lieutenant Inman, the Atholl family paid particular attention; an attention which every individual on the island seemed anxious to emulate. Perhaps this spot, so enchantingly delightful, both from the urbanity of its inhabitants, and the variety of its amusements, presented Lieutenant Inman with the happiest moments of his life.[56]

While Inman was enjoying the patronage of the Duke of Atholl, one of his predecessors in Douglas, Robert Parry Young, was having a far less agreeable experience. Australian historians have sometimes argued that the focus upon the *Bounty* has tended to dominate the study of British shipping entering the Pacific for the first time in large numbers in the 1780s. As a result of the attention which she has received, the *Bounty* is frequently seen as a lone sailer, and not as part of an extended burst of British shipping into these waters. From 1786 however British whalers had been exploring the southern Pacific, and more significantly, following the loss of North America as a dumping ground for prisoners, the transportation of convicts to Australia was beginning in earnest. In both cases, British merchants and shipping contractors who had lost the transatlantic commerce were the driving force in expanding into the Pacific. In the Royal Navy in time of peace, promotion could be slow, and duties often monotonous, even onerous. It was in these circumstances that Young, who had spent much of his life between Douglas and Liverpool, took command of a convict ship on the third fleet to Australia. An extract of a letter which he wrote from the *Albemarle* transport, dated 25 April 1791, describes a shocking sequence of events:

> On the 9th inst. the convicts rose upon us, with intention to massacre the Officers and Soldiers, and then take the vessel to America. Fortunately, however, they were repulsed and driven to take refuge in the hold, and in their prison room. Some of them were wounded. In the search after the ringleaders, we admitted one of them King's evidence, and he confessed the circumstances of the whole design. After they were subdued, it was unanimously agreed by the officers, myself, and the crew, that it was expedient to hang up the two ringleaders at the yardarm, which was accordingly put in execution. I imagine this punishment will deter them from any future attempt, since they have continued still, and apparently reconciled to their fate. There were no ships in sight at the time they rose. One of the ringleaders was an American. Two of the crew who were accomplices in the insurrection I have set on shore here, not

considering it safe to proceed with such treacherous villains on board the ship. We are one and all armed day and night, and keep the most vigilant look-out over the convicts; six of whom have died since our departure from England. Tomorrow we sail for St. Jago, the place of general rendezvous; there we shall stay a few days, and then then take our departure for [New] South Wales.[57]

What must have made this more harrowing for Young was the fact that, from the evidence of his will, he had his young second wife on the ship with him at the time.

* * *

Britain's attempts to woo the Emperor of China around this time may also be identified as part of the drive for expansion into the Pacific and Far East in search of new trading opportunities, following the loss of the United States. In September 1792, the British man of war HMS *Lion* left Portsmouth on a historic diplomatic mission. She carried Lord Macartney and his retinue, the British embassy to the Chinese Imperial Court. As an opportunity for adventure for a young man it could scarcely be rivalled and aboard the *Lion* as a sailor was a young Manxman, John Quilliam. He had previously been employed as a dockyard labourer in the fitting out of the ship, and must therefore have been aware of the unusual nature of the *Lion*'s mission to the east; perhaps it captured his imagination, for he volunteered for service aboard her. Interestingly he was rated on this, his first naval voyage, as AB rather than landsman, indicating that he had previous seagoing experience. Much has been written about Quilliam subsequently, but in many cases mythology and fact have become almost inseparably intertwined. A number of later sources have it that Quilliam was impressed, but his service record makes it clear that he volunteered for the navy. It may be that those sources have him confused with another man of the same surname who was indeed impressed, but now Quilliam stood on the brink of a career which would see him rise steadily through the ranks of the Georgian navy.

The Macartney embassy has been described as Britain's first glimpse of China. It was the first full diplomatic mission to that country, but already the trading potential of this great eastern empire was understood. Full exploitation of that potential lay some years into the future however, because as the embassy set off, Britain was on the eve of another war with France. For Quilliam, the coming war would provide the opportunity for advancement that would enable this young Manxman to make his name and fortune. One of the main protagonists involved in the *Bounty* mutiny, William Bligh, would also go on to have a distinguished career in the coming conflict. He took part in a number of subsequent naval actions, eventually reaching the rank of Vice Admiral, though his period as Governor of the colony of New South Wales was marred by another mutiny. As far as is known he never returned to the Isle of Man, though his sister-in-law Ann Bethem lived at the Hague, Onchan for a number of years. Fletcher Christian is believed to have died on Pitcairn but Peter Heywood resumed his naval career and after a spell in HMS *Queen Charlotte*, much of his later service was to be spent in the waters of the East Indies.

This new period of conflict would see the rapid expansion of the navy, providing enormous opportunities for skilled career sailors such as John Quilliam. As for Britain as a whole, she was about to be plunged into more than twenty years of almost continuous war, with a powerful and dangerous enemy which proselytised a philosophy and ideology that struck fear into the hearts of the British establishment. As well as developing modern approaches to military matters, with the state geared towards total war and huge armies raised by conscription (or *levée en masse*), France was dangerous because it exported radical ideas. The possibility of these ideas finding fertile soil in discontented parts of the United Kingdom was an abiding worry for the British state, yet with the notable exception of Ireland, most of her citizens would respond in patriotic fashion by raising volunteers and militias. Above all, the 'wooden walls' of the Royal Navy stood as a barrier against the ever present threat of French invasion.

Chapter 4

The French Revolutionary Wars

The revolutionary chaos within France following the events of 1789 led many of her European neighbours to plot against her, either in support of royalist forces in France or in order cynically to take advantage of her state of weakness. Austria and Prussia made a joint declaration in favour of the French King Louis XVI, and threatened reprisals if he was harmed. This enraged radical politicians in France, who declared war on them in response. Early French Republican successes on the battlefield, and the subsequent execution of Louis and his wife Marie Antoinette, greatly alarmed the British in turn. Great Britain also issued an ultimatum against France, and expelled her ambassador. The revolutionary leaders, having just executed a king, were in no mood to be dictated to by another monarchy just across the Channel, and on 1 February 1793 Great Britain was once again at war. The declaration of hostilities against her by the French Republic caught Great Britain at a disadvantage. Not only had she disbanded most of the newly raised regiments of 1776-1783 after the American conflict had ended, but had also reduced her regular peacetime establishment to practically nil.

Only afloat was Britain in any way prepared for war. Her navy had remained at sea in a state of readiness since the Spanish Armament of 1790, and so the outbreak of hostilities with France this time found it in a much stronger position than that at the beginning of the American war. On that occasion the navy had taken a considerable time to come up to full strength, an unfortunate situation which had hampered both military operations and the delivery of supplies. By contrast, in 1793, her dockyards were already bustling with activity, turning out cannon, shot and sail.

The only remaining problem was in manning the numerous ships of the line. Trained sailors were in short supply, and in the coming conflict the press gangs would be forced to take many men with no previous sea-going experience. This naval manpower shortage was a constant problem, which was only really resolved towards the end of the French Revolutionary war.

One of the first indications on the Isle of Man of the renewed state of hostilities came when Lieutenant Henry Inman, the naval officer in command of the *Pigmy* was suddenly removed into HMS *Victory*. The *Victory* was the flagship of the Commander-in-chief, then proceeding for Toulon, where the Royal Navy was assisting French royalists. Likewise in February 1793, some fifty men who had been enlisted by Lieutenant Samuel Cable, the naval recruiting officer in Douglas, left for Liverpool aboard the brig *Ann*. Throughout the spring of that year, Lieutenant Cable placed advertisements in the Manx newspapers offering generous bounties to able seamen, if they would enlist voluntarily in the navy. One advert in particular sought recruits for HMS *Duke*, which was under the command of the Honourable George Murray, the uncle of the Duke of Atholl.

Hugh Crow had by this stage become heavily involved in the African trade, and had spent much of the preceding three years at the kingdom of Bonny where slaves were procured. He was now second mate of the *Jane* of Liverpool, belonging to William Boats, one of the leading slave traders in Britain. Crow recalled that on receiving the news of the outbreak of war with France, the crew's first action was to prepare and indeed increase the strength of the armament of the ship:

> Having completed our cargo of about four hundred blacks we set sail, after a stay at Bonny of five months, during which we lost several of our crew, and some slaves. We proceeded towards Dominica to receive orders, but just before we made the island we were brought to by H.M. frigate *Blanche*, and informed that England was at war with France, and had taken the island of Tobago. We therefore lost no time in getting our guns, twelve in number, on deck, and having abundance

of ammunition we were soon in a condition to defend the ship, should she be attacked by the French privateers. From Dominica we proceeded to Montego bay, where we disposed of our cargo. Having procured some additional guns, and made the ship look as dashing as possible, we sailed for England in April, 1793, and came through the gulph passage without molestation.[58]

The backwards and forwards capture and re-capture of merchant ships by privateers is illustrated by a letter from Joseph Willoughby, in the Western Ocean to his father Edward Willoughby of Douglas, in March 1793:

> Having sailed from Liverpool 9th instant we this day fell in with a French privateer of 14 guns and 75 men, which a few days before had taken a brig belonging to Hull, from Dominica, homeward bound, which we have just now re-taken and sent into Liverpool. We gave chase to the privateer for three hours, but owing to her being very far to windward of us, we lost her.[59]

In spite of the state of war, Liverpool thronged with slave ships, or Guineamen as they were known. It was noted that five of the best-known such ships in that port at this time were commanded by Manxmen: the *Trelawney* under Captain Harrison, the *Ann & Susanna*, Captain Quill, the *James* under Captain Wilkes, the *Hope* under Captain Taylor, and the *John* under Captain Cowle. However, perhaps the most prominent of the Liverpool captains was John Tobin of Middle. In 1793 he was master of the Liverpool privateer *Gipsy*, and later in his career he was captain of the slaver *Molly*, which also doubled as a privateer. In both these vessels he made numerous captures. In later life, he settled as a merchant in Liverpool, concentrating upon the African slave and palm oil trade. He also continued the lucrative business of privateering, albeit from the safer position of owner rather than master. Another letter to a recipient in

Douglas from Liverpool recounted how difficult it could be to hold on to a prize once captured:

> The *Mary* Letter of Marque Guineaman, commanded by Captain Cannell (a native of your island) belonging to the owners of the *Dudgeon*, has taken a very valuable prize, and brought her into Milford; and the *Ann* privateer of 24 guns belonging to the same owners, has taken and brought in here the French privateer brig called *la Perkin* of Nantes, carrying 10 four pounders and 90 men, and being well provided with small arms, boarding nettings, pikes & c. She had been out three days and had taken nothing. Mr John Little of your town was put on board as prize-master; and 18 Frenchmen being put on board the *Ann*, the remaining 72 were all put in irons in the hold of the French privateer before the *Ann* parted her. Mr. Little had no more than 8 men allowed him to conduct the vessel home, and it was not without the greatest difficulty and close watching, and threatening to throw boiling water on them if they stirred, that he prevented them from rising.[60]

The port of Douglas meanwhile was also as busy and bustling as it ever had been before this latest Anglo-French war, indeed perhaps it was more so. In the second week of June, as well as the arrival of the weekly packet *Fly* carrying mail, and other vessels carrying timber or fish, newspapers reported the arrival and departure of the *Princess Elizabeth*, a customs cutter from Greenock which was actually a captured smuggling vessel, and which was reported to be uncommonly fast. When she left Douglas for her home port, she fired a seven-gun salute.

Another visitor to the port that week was the brig *Richard*, a Douglas vessel under Captain James Cosnahan. She had sailed from Leghorn, and her arrival confounded reports that she had been taken by a French privateer, much to the joy of the inhabitants of Douglas. Although quarantine rules prevented him from landing, Cosnahan conversed with some people who had gone out onto the rocks in the bay. He revealed that there was some substance to the rumour for he had been chased off Cape Clear by a French privateer, and had made his escape only because the enemy broke off the chase to engage easier prey.

The town of Peel was at this time inundated with beggars and vagrants from Ireland, so much so that it became necessary to remind the masters of vessels bringing them in, that they could be compelled to repatriate them. A disincentive for the Irish themselves to stay was the fact that Lieutenant John Fleming of the Impress Service (as the press gang was formally known) on the Island was quick to compel them into the welcoming arms of the senior service. Despite the prevalence of privateers on the British side, being aboard such a vessel as a crewman was no guarantee against impressment into the Royal Navy. In September 1793, the privateer *William* under Captain Philips of Castletown was at anchor in Derbyhaven. The frigate HMS *Adamant*, which had been anchored in Douglas, drew up alongside of her and sent out a pinnace. Despite the fact that some of the *William*'s crew tried to evade the press gang by jumping into the sea and swimming for the shore, their escape was made impossible by armed troops from the Royal Manx Fencibles who lined the edge of the bay, and the *Adamant* succeeded in taking some thirty men, almost the entire crew of the *William*.

At this time, impressment was carried out in a rather ad hoc fashion, and in fact Fleming had often tended to try to use carrot rather than stick wherever possible. He had started a subscription fund among the wealthy citizens of the Island, from which to pay additional bonuses to seamen who enlisted voluntarily. Indeed, he was later accused by Samuel Cable in a letter to the Admiralty of being deficient in his duty by not impressing men when he had the chance. Matters were about to change, however, and impressment would begin to take on a more organised nature following the passing of Prime Minister Pitt's Quota Act. This law stated that every district in the British Isles had to provide a certain number of men for the navy, according to its population. Despite the fact that the Keys believed the Act did not apply to the Island, the figure for the Isle of Man was set at 126.

The chief reason for which seamen were needed in such numbers was to enforce the British blockade of French ports. Royal Navy ships patrolled the waters off the coast of France, preventing food and supplies from reaching her. In order for this blockade to be effective, large numbers of ships were needed. The first and largest fleet to fleet naval action of the war was to come the following year, as a result of this policy. The British Channel fleet, under its commander Admiral Lord Howe, was positioned off Brest, expecting the arrival of a major French convoy from the United States. By the early spring of 1794, the food situation in France was desperate. With famine looming after the failure of the harvest, the French government was forced to look overseas for sustenance. Turning for supplies to France's colonies in the Americas, and to the harvests of the United States, the National Convention gave orders for the formation of a large convoy of sailing vessels to gather at Hampton Roads in the Chesapeake Bay, where French Admiral Vanstabel would wait for them. According to one contemporary historian this conglomeration of ships was said to number around 117 merchant vessels plus additional French warships for protection. The convoy had also been augmented by the United States government, in both cargo and shipping, as repayment for French financial, moral and military support during the American Revolution. The French Atlantic Fleet was to protect it when it reached French waters.

Howe's forces crossed and re-crossed the Bay of Biscay, and sent forays out into the Atlantic as they sought the expected French convoy. First to make contact with the merchant ships deep in the Atlantic were the French, whose scouts had evaded the British, but on 25 May the battle which was to culminate in the Glorious First of June began in earnest, as Howe gave chase to a French straggler who led him directly to the main enemy force. It was normal in fleet actions of the eighteenth century for the two lines of battle to pass one another sedately, exchanging fire at long ranges and then turning away, often without either side losing a ship or taking an enemy. In contrast, this time Howe was counting on the professionalism of his captains and crews combined with the advantage of the wind direction to attack the French directly, driving through their line.

This time Howe ordered each of his ships to turn individually towards the French line, intending to breach it at every point and rake the French ships at both bow and stern. The British captains would then pull up on the leeward side of their opposite numbers, cutting them off from their retreat downwind, and engage them directly, hopefully forcing each to surrender and consequently destroying the French Atlantic fleet. Among those who were present at this action was Peter Heywood of Douglas, reinstated in the Royal Navy and now serving aboard Howe's flagship HMS *Queen Charlotte,* a 100-gun first-rate. In a letter to a friend afterwards he wrote:

> At 3 oclock the next morning (29th) we got Sight of the Enemy to Windward on the starbd Tack ... Though there was a very fresh Gale & Head sea our Ships carried a great Press of Sail to get up with the Enemy, and our Van being at 7 pretty far advanced the Headmost Ship was ordered to Tack as did the Fleet in succession, and by 5 Minutes past 8 had the Line formed on the Larbd Tack. The Enemy now wore in Succession so that the two Fleets were standing on Courses parallel to each other; but as our ships hugg'd their Wind very close, and they at times edged away, they soon droppd within random Shot & began to fire, and at 10 it became brisk between five of their Van and the Ships ahead of the *Charlotte*. At 45 Mints past we hoisted our Colours and the Union at the Main, & at 4 Mints past 11 one of their Admiral Ships in the Rear [*Terrible*] carried away her fore topmast and force topsail Yard, but at the same time observed a large ship [*Trente-et-un Mai*] join them & haul into the line, consisting of 26 Ships.

Howe now realised that the enemy had no intention of engaging in a general fleet action and indeed could choose to keep the British at their distance. He decided to try to force the French ships into battle, and thus gave the signal for his ships to tack and cut the enemy line. Through the smoke and haze not every ship received the signal, at least not right away, and the turn was ragged. Only some British ships followed the instruction, some of the British captains even deliberately choosing to ignore it, but Heywood aboard the *Queen Charlotte* continues:

> About 20 Minutes past 1 observing that the *Queen, Orion, Invincible, Valiant* and *Leviathan* had tackd, we did the same followed by the *Bellerophon* our next astern, and keeping our Wind as close as possible, with the Main tack aboard, passed to Leeward of the French Admiral, then stretch along the Enemy's Line, receiving and returning the Fire, untill we forced and cut through their Line, supported by the *Bellerophon*, the only ship that followed us, the rest of our ships passing to leeward of those of the Enemy we had cut off.
>
> On our getting through & obtaining the weather Gage of the Enemy, we tackd and gave chace to a three decked Ship (bearing an Admiral's Flag) & left two disabled Ships [*Tyrannicide, Indomptable*] to be brought to by our Ships astern, but she being not much hurt attained the Centre of her own Fleet before we could bring her to action, and as they had all formed on the Starbd Tack (we then on the Larb) and were stretching on to protect their disabled Ships, we were obliged to ware and stand down to support the *Queen* who was much cut up, & the disabled Enemy's Ships joind their Fleet Without its being in our Power to prevent them, as the rest of our Ships were not near enough to give us Assistance had we attempted it. As soon as we got within random Shot of the enemy they wore and stood large, with the larb'd tacks aboard, Keeping up a constant fire at us as they passed, to which We made no Return Owing to its blowing pretty fresh with a heavy Sea. Our lower Gun deck during most of the Time we were in Action was full of water & the Pumps kept constantly going so that it

was only at intervals that the lower Deckers could be used to advantage and without endangering the Ships.[61]

During the early stages of the battle, Heywood's uncle and mentor Thomas Pasley, now a Rear Admiral and squadron commander aboard HMS *Bellerophon*, became a casualty when she was engaged in an unequal battle with two French ships. Her fore and main topmasts were shot away and another ship was forced to take her in tow. Pasley lost a leg to a cannon shot, a severe wound for any man, let alone one aged 60, and was taken below decks for treatment. He would have been tended by another Manxman, Thomas Fargher the ship's surgeon, who came from Shenvalla. For his services on this day Pasley received a baronetcy and a pension of £1000 a year, but he almost certainly owed his life to Fargher's skill. A friendship seems to have been forged between them, for it was at Pasley's house near Winchester that Fargher passed away, just a few months later. The *Bellerophon* was known to her crew as the 'Billy Ruffian', and one of the Midshipmen aboard her at this time was William Frissell. Born in 1776, Frissell had already been in the Royal Navy three years by this point, having first gone aboard HMS *Perseus* as an able seaman. He was a son of John Frissell, High Bailiff of Ramsey and member of the House of Keys. Two of Frissell's brothers would also serve in the Royal Navy, and they were clearly a seafaring family, for an uncle Henry Frissell had died at St Kitts in the 1750s whilst in command of the Liverpool trader *Juno*. Despite the name, the battle of the Glorious First of June was an inconclusive affair, with both sides claiming victory. In fact, both fleets had been so badly damaged in the action that neither was in a position to continue with offensive operations in the short term. Most of the convey succeeded in getting through, so the French could at least claim a moral victory.

The previous year Hugh Crow, in the slave ship *Gregson*, had been taken prisoner by a French privateer whilst on the first leg of a journey to Guernsey to collect spirits and then on to West Africa. Having been held captive in deplorable conditions in a number of French prisons, he resolved to try to win his freedom. In this effort, his knowledge of Manx played a significant role:

> My spirits now began to rally, and I went to work to plan my escape. With this view I formed a vocabulary, in my mind, of all the French words I could pick up, and about the beginning of May, 1795, when the weather had become fine, I contrived to elude the vigilance of my keepers, and, having first fixed in my hat a large tri-coloured cockade, I took the road from Pontoise, my object being to gain some port whence I might find a passage to England. I made a pretty favourable departure; but next day, when I had proceeded about fifty miles on my way, I was intercepted at a bridge by an officer and a file of soldiers. I was strictly interrogated, but in my confusion I had forgotten nearly all my French, and stood mute. The officer followed up one stern inquiry by another, but all to no purpose. At length, as a random expedient, I bolted out all the words of the different languages I could remember, and of which I had obtained a smattering in my different voyages, mingling the whole with my native language, the Manks, with a copiousness proportioned to my facility in speaking it. The Frenchman was astonished and enraged, and as he went on foaming and roaring, I continued to repeat (in broken Spanish) 'No entiendo!' – until worn out of all patience, he swore I was a Breton, and giving me a sharp slap with his sword, he exclaimed 'Vat en, coquin!' I thanked him over and over again, as loud as I could, in Manks, and I assure the reader never were thanks tendered with more sincerity.[62]

Crow returned to Liverpool, where one of the first people he met was his brother William, also a mate aboard a slave ship. Both Crow brothers were shortly to sail again for Bonny to collect slaves, and on the middle passage

An eighteenth century engraving showing captives being rowed out to a slave ship on the coast of West Africa. (Library of Congress)

A contemporary cartoon showing the humiliation of a slave girl who had refused to dance for the ship's crew.

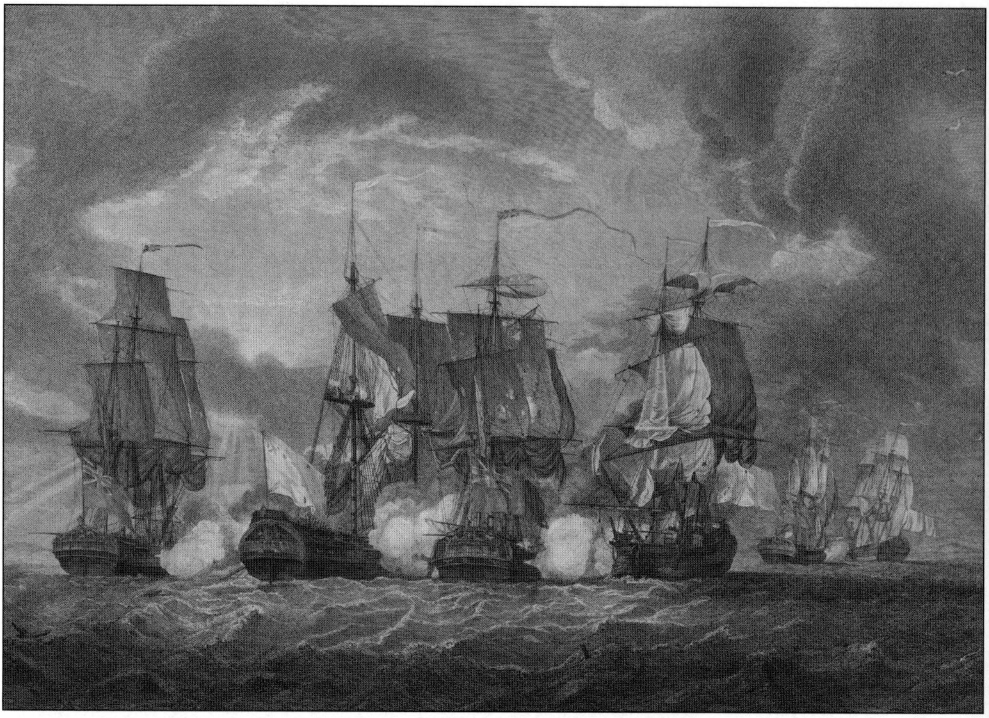

TO BE SOLD, on board the Ship *Bance-Yſland*, on tueſday the 6th of *May* next, at *Aſhley-Ferry*; a choice cargo of about 250 fine healthy

NEGROES,

juſt arrived from the Windward & Rice Coaſt. —The utmoſt care has already been taken, and ſhall be continued, to keep them free from the leaſt danger of being infected with the SMALL-POX, no boat having been on board, and all other communication with people from *Charles-Town* prevented.

Auſtin, Laurens, & Appleby.

N. B. Full one Half of the above Negroes have had the SMALL-POX in their own Country.

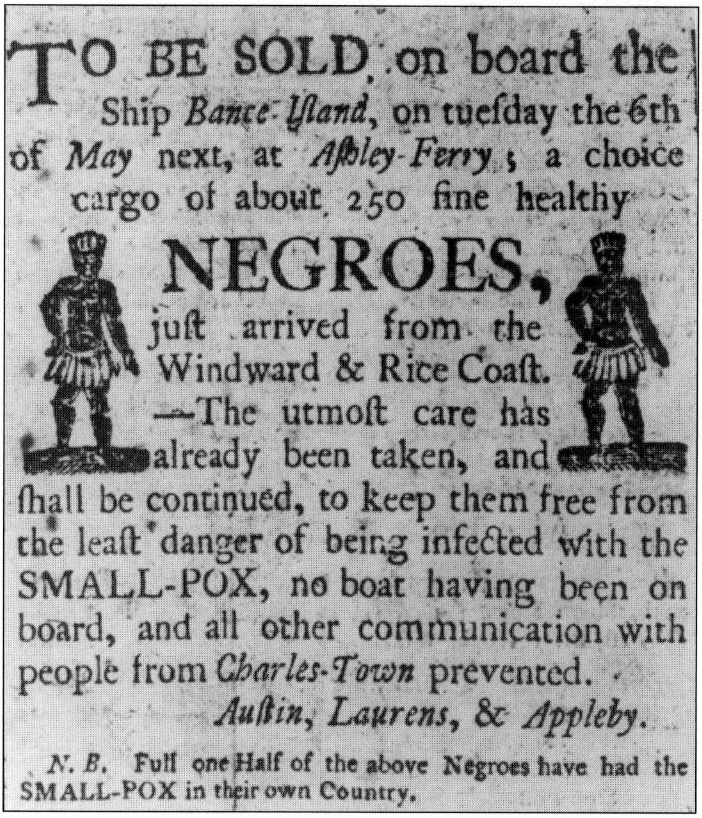

Above: *The Battle off the Point of Ayre, Isle of Man, February 1760. This action saw the French squadron of François Thurot defeated.*

Left: *An advertisement for the sale of slaves on the South Carolina coast, 1770s.*

Captain James Cook, the navigator who mapped the Pacific and Australasia for the first time. (Library of Congress)

Above: *The death of Captain James Cook in Hawaii. (Library of Congress)*

Below: *A Royal Navy frigate at Southampton, 1786 by Dominic Serres.*

John Paul Jones, father of the United States Navy, and menace of the Irish Sea in the 1780s. (Library of Congress)

French Admiral de Grasse, who defeated the British at the Battle of the Chesapeake. (Library of Congress)

A portrait of slave trader Hugh Crow, from the frontispiece of his memoirs.

To all GENTLEMEN SEAMEN, whofe Hearts glow with Ardour for the Honour of the *Isle of Man, Whitehaven,* and the other Ports in *Cumberland.*

NOW fitting out at DOUGLAS, *Isle of Man,* againft the French and Americans, then to proceed to MONTEGO BAY in JAMAICA and return to the *Isle of Man,*

THE SHIP

T Y G E R,

Capt. Qualtrough,

Who ferved his Time and was Mate for 11 Years with Capt. ISAAC BARRAE, a Gentleman well known here, whofe Abilities and Courage do Honour to the Gentlemen Seamen who were in his Employ. Mounts 16 Guns, Swivels, &c. Carries 70 Men, and a fafe Protection for all the Crew. All Gentlemen Seamen who are defirous to enrich themfelves upon the Spoils of the French and Americans, and willing to embark on this Voyage will receive FULL WAGES, together with ONE QUARTER of all PRIZES, which will be fhared among them immediately upon Condemnation, let them repair to Mr. William Haile's the George, on the Cuftom Houfe Quay, where they will meet with the greateft Encouragement from Capt. Richard Qualtrough.

GOD fave the KING.

Succefs to the TYGER and all her BRAVE CREW.

An advertisement for crewmen for the Manx-owned privateer Tyger. *It offers protection from impressment to the crew, but this was to prove false.*

Commodore George Johnstone, Royal Navy. He impressed most of the crew of the unfortunate Tyger. (RMG/Public Domain Image)

Captain William Locker, by Dominic Serres. He was a mentor to the young Horatio Nelson and also Manx officer, Robert Cottier. (Yale Centre for British Art)

A Royal Navy sailor on shore leave, with prize money to spend. This 1795 image provides a good illustration of naval uniform at the time.

Right: *Lieutenant William Bligh, who began his naval career in Douglas, Isle of Man, and there met two of the other main protagonists in the Mutiny on the Bounty.*

Below: *Bligh and the loyalists are set adrift in an open boat, following the Mutiny on the Bounty, 1789.*

Above: *HMS* Pandora *sinking on the Great Barrier Reef, as sketched by Peter Heywood.*

Left: *Captain Henry Inman, who commanded the cutter HMS* Pygmy *at Douglas in 1790.*

Above: *The Battle of the Glorious First of June, 1794.*

Right: *An appeal for naval recruits from the Regulating Officer for Douglas, Lieutenant Clark, 1803.*

VOLUNTEERS FOR THE NAVY.

ALL ABLE SEAMEN, SEA-FARING MEN, and LANDMEN, who are willing to serve on Board His Majesty's Fleet, may repair to the

RENDEZVOUS in DOUGLAS,

Under the Direction of Lieut. JOSEPH CLARK:

They shall not only receive such Bounties as His Majesty may have thought proper to promise by His Royal Proclamation, but also Two Months Wages in advance, before the Ship or Vessel they may be appointed to serve in proceeds to Sea.

GOD SAVE THE KING.

Douglas, 28th April, 1803.

Above: *Two unwilling recruits seized by a press gang. The man on the right may be an innkeeper, holding his hand out to the Lieutenant in expectation of a reward for information.*

Below: *The Battle of Trafalgar, 21 October 1805.*

Above: *Nelson lies stricken on the deck of HMS* Victory, *whilst a group of concerned officers look on. Lieutenant John Quilliam is the right-hand-most of the five.*

Below: *HMS* Shannon *and USS* Chesapeake, *locked together in action. (Library of Congress)*

Above: *The grave of Manx hero Philip Cosnahan, at Old Kirk Braddan.*

Below: *The monument to the 'Gallant Manxmen' of Trafalgar, erected in Douglas in 2005, to mark the bicentenary of the battle.*

THE FRENCH REVOLUTIONARY WARS

to Barbados, Hugh's ship the *Anne* was attacked by a French privateer, which he drove off using bags of copper dross, fired from his ship's guns in place of grape shot. This he recorded caused great injury on the decks of the enemy ship. When they eventually reached their destination, most of the men and boys on board the *Anne* were impressed by the Royal Navy, a galling reception after the way they had defended themselves. The Royal Navy however was still desperately in need of men in order to keep its fleets around the world at full strength. On 23 June 1795, Admiral Alexander Hood commanding the Channel Fleet brought the French to book once again at the Battle of Groix. The French admiral Villaret had driven off a small force of British ships on the previous day, only for Hood's large force to appear in their support. Believing that the stronger British fleet would destroy his own twelve ships of the line, Villaret ordered his force to fall back to the inshore anchorage off Groix, hoping to take shelter in the protected coastal waters. Several of his ships were too slow however, falling behind so that early in the morning of 23 June the rearmost ships of his fleet were caught by the British vanguard, overhauled one by one and brought to battle. Although Villaret fought a determined rearguard action, three French ships were captured, all with heavy casualties, and the remainder of the French fleet was left scattered across miles of coastline. In this position they were highly vulnerable to continued British attack, but after only a few hours engagement, concerned that his ships might be wrecked on the rocky shore, Hood called off the action and allowed Villaret to regroup and retreat to Lorient.

Present here aboard HMS *Russell,* a seventy-four-gun third-rate ship, was Captain Joseph Bacon of the 118th Regiment, a son of Douglas merchant John Joseph Bacon. The 118th Regiment in this period served aboard men of war as marines, and was one of those short-lived regiments which came into existence after the outbreak of war with France. It was raised in Ireland in 1794 as the Fingal Regiment, or Talbot's Regiment of Foot, and had spent a period of time in training in the Isle of Man, which is probably where Bacon joined it. The following year it transferred to Portsmouth for sea service. Later in his career Bacon wrote a memorial of his service. Referring to himself in the third person, as was common in such documents at this time, he writes:

> He did previous to his embracing his present profession (with the single assistance of a Boy) retake a vessel of his father's from nine Frenchmen when going into Brest, and brought her into Falmouth. He did in the action of the 23rd June in the exercise of a duty that has been the pride of his life receive a wound on his Head serving as Captain of Marines under Vice Admiral Lord Bridport. He has in one unbroken tenour of Loyalty supported the Character of his King as the Father of his people and all his family with that ardour and affection which their virtues create.[63]

Other accounts state that the vessel which he managed to retake on an earlier occasion was the *Christian* of Douglas, which had been under his command. She had been captured by the French frigate *Tribune* whilst on a journey from Naples to Rotterdam, and Bacon had been held prisoner aboard her. However *Lloyd's List* states that he was subsequently placed aboard another capture, the *Hibernia* of Belfast, but concurs in that he did indeed overpower the French prize crew, albeit with the assistance of two men rather than one. Bacon goes on to add that he paid 2000 guineas for his command of a company in the army, but there was perhaps also some family influence at work for one of the senior officers in this regiment in 1794 was Major John Taubman. This however was no sinecure. The 118th Regiment was to all intents and purposes destroyed at Groix, and the few survivors were transferred afterwards to another regiment. The wound he received in this action may well have contributed to his early death, for Bacon later passed away aged just 35 whilst holding a captaincy in a veteran battalion on garrison duty in Guernsey.

Another marine officer from the Isle of Man was Thomas Crebbin, who seems to have been learning his craft as an apothecary or surgeon much as his uncle (and namesake) had been before him in the Seven Years' War.

THE FRENCH REVOLUTIONARY WARS

However it was through the influence of his sister's husband, an officer in the Corps of Marines (as yet not Royal) that he had recently been accepted into the regiment. He wrote to his brother-in-law in the same month:

> I am desired by my Father who still continues very ill and confined by his old Rheumatic complaints (he himself not being very well able to write) to acknowledge the receipt of your kind favour of the 20th ins., whereby I saw that your goodness has procured me a second Lieutenancy in his Majesty's Corps of Marines. My Father desires me to return you his most sincere and grateful thanks for this distinguished mark of your goodness, and at the same time I must beg you to accept of my own, and hope that my conduct in life will so far meet with your approbation, as well as that of all my friends as to leave no room for thinking that there has been a misapplication of the favour conferr'd. Should my appearance at quarters be found necessary Dr. Scott is so good as to tell me, that should I be 3 months absent, he would allow me that time. This I take very kind of Dr. Scott, he at present having no assistant but myself, and rather than it shuld be attended with any disappointment or inconvenience to me, he would get a son of Dr. La Mothe's of Castletown, to serve him 'till I returned should the time be longer.[64]

Thomas's brother Lieutenant Paul Crebbin had been with the Marines since 1793 and was later involved in a dramatic action at sea between his own ship, the frigate HMS *Thetis,* (which was operating off the coast of North America) and a small French force. The commander of the *Thetis*, Captain Cochrane, wrote afterwards:

> I am sorry to say, that we had 8 of our best men killed, and 9 others wounded, some of them badly ... From the fire of the three rear ships being principally directed at the *Thetis*,

our rigging and sails were almost cut to pieces, our lower masts and yards shot through, which, with the other damages we received, prevented me from pursuing the enemy, and to take possession of those that had struck. To Mr. Mackie, the Master, I shall ever feel obliged for the assistance he gave me during the action. The carronades on the quarterdeck were very ably served by Lieutenant Crebbin, and the marines under his command.[65]

Numbers of Manx-born officers and sailors were now serving with the Royal Navy at sea around the world. In the following month, June 1795, British forces were heavily engaged in the Caribbean in fighting the escaped slave populations of the West Indian islands. In one action, on the island of St Vincent, Douglas man Robert Benjamin Young of the sloop HMS *Thorn* (armed with sixteen 6-pounders) made a name for himself in an amphibious operation. Previously he had taken part in the capture of the French corvette *Le Courrier National* of 18 guns (8 and 6 pounders) and 119 men which was taken after a spirited night-action of 35 minutes, with a loss to the British of no more than 6 men wounded, out of a crew of 80. The French ship suffered seven killed and 20 wounded. Now Young was engaged in a joint operation with the army, in which his ship carried a party of soldiers from the 60th Regiment to storm the outpost of Owia. Young had eight men killed and wounded in his own boat, half of them belonging to the *Thorn*, the others to the 60th Regiment. One report stated:

During the Carib war in the island of St. Vincent, Mr. Young also distinguished himself, particularly in the attacks upon Owia and Chateau Bellair, the success of the British at which places compelled the enemy to retire into the interior. At Owia, where he was opposed by 400 of the enemy, he landed (through a heavy surf) a detachment of 100 men from the 46th and 60th Regts. On this occasion his own boat, the leading one, had 8 men killed and wounded; and he himself but narrowly escaped, having had his hat and clothes shot through.[66]

Meanwhile, with the fall of the Dutch Republic to French forces, the Cape of Good Hope took on additional significance for Great Britain. It was the only place in southern Africa at which British ships making the long journey to the East Indies might stop to resupply. If the Dutch and their French masters denied it to them this would have disastrous consequences. A British expedition led by Vice Admiral Sir George Keith Elphinstone sailed in April 1795, arriving off Simon's Town at the Cape in June. Attempts were made to negotiate a settlement with the colony, but talks achieved nothing and an amphibious landing was made on 7 August. A short battle was fought at Muizenberg, and skirmishing between British and Dutch troops continued until September when a larger military force landed. With Cape Town now under threat, Dutch Governor Abraham Josias Sluysken surrendered the colony. Elphinstone subsequently strengthened the garrison against counter-attack and stationed a Royal Navy squadron off the port. A later Dutch attempt to recapture the Cape was defeated, and among those who took part in the action was William Kelly, now a Midshipman in HMS *Arrogant*. He received a silver cup in recognition of his part in this battle, and remained on the Cape for several more months, as Acting Master in both HMS *Echo* and the prize *Van Trompe*, a Dutch warship which he later brought back to Portsmouth.

Back in European waters, in late 1795, the naval career of John Quilliam began to take him beyond the realm of most men of his social class. After leaving the *Lion* upon her return from China he had been posted to HMS *Prince George*, a 98-gun first rate in the Channel Fleet, where he was promoted from Able Seaman to Quarter Master's Mate, a first rung on the career ladder. Now, in February 1796 he was serving aboard HMS *Triumph*, a ship of 74 guns and here was appointed Master's Mate. Master's Mates were allowed to command smaller vessels, walk the quarterdeck, and mess in the gunroom with the other warrant officers. Each Master's Mate took his own watch, acting as deputy to the lieutenant of that watch. Master's Mates also had to keep detailed logs similar to midshipmen. As previously noted, this was a position usually allocated to those who showed promise and who sought more responsibility, as a prelude to taking their lieutenant's exam.

In a similar situation was Edward Quayle, son of John Quayle, Clerk of the Rolls, who in 1795 had been serving as a midshipman on the Newfoundland Station aboard HMS *Ramillies,* under the command of Sir Richard Bickerton. In earlier life, Quayle had fallen into dissolute ways, but perhaps service in the navy had given him more purpose. As well as gaining valuable sailing experience, he had also been given a temporary promotion by Bickerton, to Acting Master's Mate, a position which he had been promised permanently when the vacancy arose. In a letter to his brother George Quayle he adds:

> Time will not permitt [sic] to mention more only that I am sadly at a loss for cloaths of all sorts as my stock that I had from home with me are almost entirely worn out and am almost like a Marine Dress with a needle and Undress with a knife ... We shall be both at Cadiz and Lisbon before we get home as it is expected we shall go with the convoy. Sir Richard says he wishes he could fall in with 3 or 4 more Guaney Mates to show his Boys their Duty.[67]

This last comment was a reference to treasure ships bound for Spain. Shortly afterwards Edward did indeed return to home waters. However in another letter to his brother George written aboard HMS *Ramillies,* this time at Spithead, and dated 13 February 1796 Edward states that their destination has changed from a cruise off Cádiz to the North Sea, in order to join with Admiral Duncan 'with all expedition':

> We have no appearances of a peace here every Department is as busy as possible fitting out every ship with the greatest dispatch but there is the greatest want of all kind of stores

both in the Navy & Victualling Office. Our being sent on this Station is owing to an account they have received of Ten Sail of the line having sailed from the Texel (northern Holland) to the Northward so that if we fall in with them [we] may expect a hard job of it ... You must excuse the shortness of this as we are all bustle and hurry.[68]

The veteran Admiral Adam Duncan commanded the North Sea Fleet based at Great Yarmouth, its duty being to blockade the Dutch fleet of twenty ships in its base at Texel. With the losses it had sustained the previous year in the Atlantic, the French Republican fleet had instructed the subservient Dutch to combine with them at Brest. It was imperative that the British keep the Dutch bottled up in their harbour, and Duncan's scratch force made up of older vessels and ships from reserve, was given this task. The Dutch however were not the only opponents at sea, French privateers continued to cause problems, particularly in the West Indies. Captain Radcliffe Shimin was one of a family of merchant captains from Maughold. Like many Manx officers he sailed out of Liverpool, often on the slave routes and in one incident, which he describes in a letter on 30 November 1796, he actually armed his slaves to fight off the French:

On the 28th instant, about forty leagues to the eastward of Barbadoes, at daylight in the morning, we fell in with a large French schooner, of 12 guns; after giving him a broad-side, he bore away. Same day – at meridian, rather hazy, saw a ship to the S.W. standing to the northward, about six miles distant. As we got nearer, perceived her to be a ship of force. Did not like her appearance, but found it impossible to avoid her, and to induce him to shew colours, hauled our wind, hoisted an ensign, and fired a gun to windward. On which, he hauled up his courses, down stay sails, and fired two guns to windward, then hoisted the bloody flag – at the fore-top-gallant masthead. We then saw what he was; kept our wind, which he perceiving, made after us. Finding my people all healthy and well disposed (particularly my officers), and with the assistance of the best of our slaves, prepared for action, and about two o'clock he got along-side of us, hoisted his French ensign, and before there was any time for hailing, gave us a broadside, which we returned warmer than he wished. The action continued without ever ceasing, till five o'clock, when he sheered off, and stood to the northward.

The only damage we received was in our sails and rigging; not a man hurt. She was as handsome a frigate-built ship as I have seen, mounted 20 guns, nine-pounders, on her main deck, and eight guns on her quarter deck; had much the appearance of the *Princess Royal*, formerly of Liverpool. My people were in high spirits, and if we could have got alongside of him again, we would, I am certain, have saved them the trouble of taking down their bloody flag, but our rigging and sails being a good deal cut, partly prevented us. He was much more shattered than us, and his hull pretty well moth eaten, his quarter was at one time so well cleared, with our eighteen-pounders, that we suppose a number of them slept under their arms. Nothing but his superior sailing saved him at last. We expended five barrels of gun-powder, and the next afternoon, about five o'clock, made the Island of Barbadoes.[69]

The ship which Shimin commanded was the *Tarleton*, belonging to Messrs. Tarleton and Rigg, of Liverpool, and his actions in arming the slaves to fight the French was an extremely risky one, given the numbers of insurrections which had taken place aboard slave ships in the past, and about which he must certainly have known. Nevertheless it was not a unique incident, for Hugh Crow records in his memoirs that he also armed some slaves for defence against the French on a passage a few years after this, even going so far as to give them a rudimentary uniform of cap, shirt and trousers. Shimin in addition to the *Tarleton* captained the *Toms*, *Prince of Wales*, and *King George*. He is also on record as having commanded a number of privateers in this era. He died at Ramsey five years later, having retired from the sea and having recently married a 17-year-old of good birth named Mary Tellet.

The entry of Spain into the war on the side of France in October 1796 had made the British position in the Mediterranean untenable, as the combined Franco-Spanish fleet in those waters now outnumbered the British by more than two to one. Early in 1797, the Spanish fleet set sail to rendezvous with their French counterparts at Brest. If the two fleets were to combine it would have made for a formidable force, and thus the British under Admiral Sir John Jervis with ten ships (and five reinforcements on the way) attempted to intercept them. Despite the fact that he was outnumbered, tackling the Spanish fleet alone was clearly preferable to allowing the Spanish and French to combine. Jervis encountered the Spaniards in thick fog off Cape St Vincent, Portugal on 14 February 1797. Even though he had no idea how many ships he was up against, Jervis felt it was imperative that he attack at once. The Spanish ships were in two loose groups whilst Jervis quickly got his into a line. The British at least had the advantage that they were prepared for battle and the enemy were not. One of the smaller ships in the British force was the sloop HMS *Bonne Citoyenne* in which Douglas-born Robert Benjamin Young was now serving. As well as seeing active service in this battle, Young was severely contused some weeks afterwards in an attack made, in company with a squadron under Lord Garlies, on a Spanish ship of the line off Cape de Gata, when he was struck by part of his ship's foretopmast, shot away during the contest.

In October 1797, after having been blockaded at Texel throughout the summer, a number of Dutch ships under Admiral Jan de Winter finally put to sea. Whether they hoped to fall upon a smaller British force and overwhelm it, or sneak past the English coast and join the French is not clear. However the odds were against the Dutch. Their crews were less experienced than the British, who were also better trained. Furthermore, de Winter had doubts about the loyalty and morale of his men. Being cooped up in port for so long had been bad for the latter, and many Dutch people had no liking for the French Republic.

Admiral Duncan's reinforced fleet divided roughly in half, and the two columns proceeded to engage the Dutch in what became the Battle of Camperdown, one of the hardest fought naval engagements of the French Revolutionary Wars and certainly the severest action fought between the British and the Dutch. The latter put up a determined fight and they emulated the British practice of firing at the hull rather than the rigging and masts of an enemy, which produced heavy casualties on the gun decks. John Quilliam was present at this action aboard HMS *Triumph*, and afterwards was promoted to the rank of Acting Lieutenant, a post he was to hold for a month before returning to the rank of Master's Mate. The following year, after completing the necessary six years in the Royal Navy, Quilliam applied for examination for the permanent rank of Lieutenant.

By 1798 the rapid expansion of the Royal Navy which characterised the early years of the Revolutionary war had levelled off. The manpower problems of those early days had also largely been resolved by the Quota Acts, but more importantly by the improvements in naval pay which followed the mutinies of the previous year. A clear spike in volunteer enlistment afterwards is largely attributable to these reforms. Nevertheless Samuel Cable was at pains to expand his operations in the Isle of Man, and his eye fell upon the herring fleet as a potential source of new recruits. In spite of the disaster of eleven years earlier, the Isle of Man remained heavily dependent upon herring both as a source of food and, since the demise of the running trade, as a source of revenue. Feltham gives an interesting description of the fishing fleet in his account from 1798, writing:

> The boat-builders are uncommonly clever, constructing entirely by the eye, making no use of line or rule, unless in laying the keel. The Manks boats are in size from 23 to 33 feet in keel; and 13 feet beam, with 6 feet hold; they are cutter-rigged, sail remarkably fast, and withstand a heavy sea ... Manks boats seldom exceed eight tons, and cost, including

the nets, about 70 guineas. The produce is divided into nine shares; two for the owner of the boat; one for the proprietor of the nets; the other six to the fishermen. The nets are buoyed up by inflated bags of dog-skin dried in the sun, and smeared over with tar. Upwards of 400 boats compose the Manks fleet. An admiral and vice-admiral are annually elected the one is allowed £5 by government, the other £2 for the season. These conduct the fleet to the herring ground. On leaving the harbour the fishermen, with uncovered heads invoke the blessing of Providence; and Bishop Wilson's Form of Prayer for the Herring Fishery, is used during the season ... The fishermen sometimes exorcise, or burn the witches out of their boats with dry ring, or heath; and to eject this they contrive the flame so as to reach every part of the boat. The first boat that discovers the herring, sounds a horn as a signal to apprise the other boats. They sometimes take 70 maize, at 500 per maize, in one boat.[70]

These fishermen however presented too tempting a target for Captain Samuel Cable, the Regulating Officer or commander of the Impress Service at Douglas. His recruiting station, as in any British port, was called the Rendezvous. It was often located at an inn, and was usually decorated with flags and bunting in order to make it conspicuous. It is known that for a time at least, Cable lived with his wife and daughter on Duke Street in Douglas, and his Rendezvous may well have been on the same street. The Rendezvous had been closed since the previous December, during which time the Island had become, in Cable's words, an asylum for seamen from Liverpool, anxious to avoid the Impress in that port. However it was the services of the Manx fishermen which Cable was now most eager to secure for His Majesty's Navy. He wrote to his masters at the Admiralty in June 1798:

> I ... beg leave to submit to their Lordships' consideration that there are between four and five hundred large boats in this Island, employed in the herring fishery, each of which has

seven men or more belonging to them. A man or two taken from each of these Boats would be an excellent supply to the Navy, but it is utterly impossible for any Gang stationed here to perform this service. The means I would recommend to effect this business, is by ordering some of the Frigates and Cutters employed on the Irish coast opposite this Island to cruise round it and when they perceive the fleet of Herring boats, two or three Leagues from land (which they are every day when the weather is moderate) the Frigates then might cut them of [sic], and take a man out of each Boat, which would neither distress the Island, nor the Fishery. The men so procured, would in a short time make very good seamen, when mixed with others on board his Majesty's Navy, they being very quiet, and not in the least given to Mutiny. If their Lordships think proper to adopt this scheme they will have the goodness to order the commander of such Frigates and other vessels they may send on this service, to correspond with me on the subject as I can inform them when the most proper time will be to carry it into execution. The height of the herring fishing is just at hand.[71]

The resistance of the Manx people to any interference with the fishing industry, which was one of the chief sources of income for the Island was considerable yet Cable continued with his efforts to have the herring crews impressed. He wrote again to the Admiralty in the following month, informing them of the opposition locally to forced enlistment of the fishermen, yet still he persisted in advising the Lords Commissioners that they should proceed with the plan:

> ... from what I understand happened yesterday, at the annual Court of Tynwald, it does not appear that the Deemsters who are the Chief Civil Magistrates of the Island will suffer any Press Gang to impress a single Manx Fisherman out of any boat

so employed. And the Keys likewise shewed great aversion to the measure. Under these circumstances the only method of procuring a considerable supply of men from this place will be by the means I mentioned in my last and by which I think three or four Hundred may be procured, by a general sweep. These men are, from their infancy employed for some part of the year on the water, so that there will be little trouble in making them tolerably good Seamen; indeed many of them are so already, having been brought up on board the larger smacks employed in the coasting trade from the Island. The boats employed in the herring fishing are from twelve to two or three and twenty tons burthen and are cutter rigg'd [sic], so that the people in them must of course be infinitely better than any Landsman; and I cannot help pointing these out, as well worth the attention of their Lordships. There are upwards of three thousand men employed in these boats.[72]

Cable was to get his wish, for shortly afterwards Lieutenant Richard Harrison, a commander of transports on the south coast, arrived in Manx waters with his vessel HMS *Spider*. On this occasion the Manx fishermen faced another threat beyond those customary ones of the weather and the sea with which they were regularly acquainted. That evening the boats of the Royal Navy sloop came amongst them as they worked, taking men and boys alike for the service of the King. In Douglas the following day there was great consternation over the incident, with much of the anger of the townsfolk understandably directed at Samuel Cable. He reported this to his masters, adding that such was the level of agitation he was forced to promise that no more men would be taken from the herring fleet. He wrote a further letter to the Admiralty on 16 September 1798 in which he stated:

... in consequence of the Manx fishermen being impressed by the *Spider*, the country has been in a constant state of fermentation. The mob have made use of violent threats, and have even gone so far as to talk of Tarring and Feathering me. As this commotion does not seem likely to subside soon, I should be greatly obliged to their Lordships would please to remove me to any part of Great Britain, where I might stand a chance of being made useful, the first vacancy that offers ... I beg further to report to their Lordships that I have received great support from Lieutenant Governor Shaw, who has done everything in his power to protect His Majesty's Service from insult and indignity.[73]

Yet on the same day he wrote to a friend in England, playing down both his part in impressing the men, and the drama of the reaction which followed:

In the first place I have to inform you that I am alive, which is what I cou'd not have promis'd you at this time a week ago, for at that time my life was threatened by more than one. In order that you may the better understand this business you are to know that some time since, my very good masters, the Lords Commissioners of the Admiralty, sent a Vessel here for the purpose of Impressing a number of Men out of the Manx Herring Boats, they having been inform'd by somebody, that several thousands were employed in that Trade, and that there was no apparent reason why a Manx Fisherman shou'd not be as liable to the Impress as an English one. I suppose their Lordships were convinced by these arguments, for they ordered the *Spider*, Schooner, commanded by a Lieut. Harrison to proceed on this Station for the above purpose, and last Friday Night, but one (dreadful to relate) he carried their orders into effect by impressing about fifty of those sacred persons. Had an Earthquake happen'd or any other Convulsion of Nature, it cou'd not have had a more terrible effect on the Inhabitants of this Isle. That they were entirely ruin'd was past a doubt, and that this ruinous business was occasioned by Captain Cable was another truth which no one cou'd pretend to deny. His throat, of course, ought to be cut at least, and his House pulled about his ears. In the meantime he, honest man, showed no concern nor took any precautions about the matter. The bustle is now, I believe a little subsided, & there has been no throats cutt, nor any houses pull'd down. The Keys have, however, had a meeting about the business, and they have memorialised the Admiralty representing I suppose that the persons of their fishermen ought to be held sacred, and demanding that this terrible business shou'd be no more repeated. And now you have got a history of the most eventful circumstance that ever happened to the Isle of Man.[74]

Cable's apparent disingenuousness in trying to distance himself from an unpopular incident which he had deliberately instigated is possibly explained by the fact that both Cable and his correspondent were friends with Major John Taubman. In spite of his protests to the contrary, Cable had almost certainly underestimated the strength of the reaction that the wholesale impressment of fishermen would cause, and was probably concerned that Taubman and the Keys should not learn too much of his involvement in it. A remarkable insight into the experiences of one of the fishermen who was impressed on this occasion comes from a fragile calfskin journal kept by one of them, a man named Thomas Callister of Jurby. In it he records phonetically the old pronunciation of Port Erin, stating that:

> ... In the year of our Lord God 1798 I was pressed by the *Spider* schooner off Port Iron Bay the 8th Day of September '98. We saild [sic] from Port Iron the 9th of Septr and came to an anchor in Milford 13th Septr and saild for Plymouth the 20th of Septr and came to Anchor in Plymouth 22nd of the

same month and that same day put on bord [sic] the Slop ship and the 25 I was put on bord the *Cambridge* and then I was Drafted for HMS *Captain* and put on board HMS *Neptune* in Causand Bay Oct the 6th and saild to Torbay and was put on bord HMS *Pheaton* [sic] Frigate and then saild for Causand Bay again and the *Captain* arrived off a cruse that Day and we were put on bord of her being October the 20th 1798 and Saild for Porthmouth the 22nd and arrived in Porthmouth 26 of Octr and Lyed at Anchor there till the 17th of Janry 1799 and sailed for a cruse from Spithead and Dropd Anchor at St Willins [?] and saild from St Willins the 28 of Jan 1799 and crused off Brest and in the Chenal [sic] till the 16 of Febry we came to anchor in torbay in a shocking gale of Wind all our Sails gone in Shivers and saild out of torbay for a Cruse the 2nd of March and Saild for Spithead April 6th and arrived in Spithead the 8th April and we sailed from Spithead the 4th of May and came to anchor in Causand Bay 5 of May and saild out of Causand Bay 6 of May and steard SW till we came to Lisbon the 16 May and came to Gibraltar the 19th of May and came to Minorca the 29th of May and joined Lord Kieth [sic] Fleet 31 May and we took 3 French Frigates and 2 Brigs in the Gulf of Lions the 18 of June then we sailed to Jersey and send the prisoners on shore.[75]

The slop ship referred to here was a vessel being used as a depot for sailors' clothes and hammocks, and here Callister would have been kitted out, with any deficiencies in clothing made good. There was no uniform as such, though sailors tended to be issued upper garments in blue, with white (or red and white) striped trousers. Any uniformity of dress came about only if the clothing had been bought in bulk. Often sailors were issued with a round brimmed straw hat, which they tarred themselves to protect it, or one made of leather. Often they would add the name of their ship in gold letters.

THE FRENCH REVOLUTIONARY WARS

It is interesting to note that just prior to Callister's joining her, HMS *Captain* had been the flagship of Admiral Lord Nelson. She was only just returning to active service after being severely damaged in battle in the Mediterranean, where Admiral George Elphinstone (Lord Keith) was now in command of British naval forces. Following the destruction of most of their warships at the Battle of the Nile, the French had attempted to regroup and regain control of the Mediterranean under Vice Admiral Étienne Eustache Bruix, whose force led Keith's on a long chase whilst also linking up with their Spanish allies. Callister's account is unusual because so few men in the lower decks could read and write. Perhaps because he was clearly a literate and reasonably well educated man, Callister seems to have held positions of some responsibility and his notebook also contains details of a naval signal code in use at this time. Again this is intriguing as unauthorised copies of code books were frowned upon by the navy, lest they should accidentally fall into enemy hands. Callister was to spend three years in the Royal Navy, and his subsequent cruises took him to the West Indies and back.

The oil which really drove the Royal Navy was prize money. The previous year, John and Thomas Quayle visited the Admiralty in London attempting, unsuccessfully, to discover more about the whereabouts of their brother Edward, as news had been received that his last known ship HMS *Legere* had captured a valuable Spanish vessel. If he had remained aboard, then the brothers felt that he might have been entitled to some prize money. A few months after this, in October 1799, John Quilliam, now a Lieutenant aboard the frigate HMS *Ethalion*, along with three other British vessels, was involved in an engagement with the Spanish treasure ship *Thetis*. In a battle lasting about an hour, in which the *Ethalion* had quickly caught up with her prey and gave her the benefit of two well directed broadsides, the Spanish ship struck her colours. She had sustained only one fatal casualty, the British ship none at all. What was more significant however was what she was carrying. In time of war, all captured enemy vessels were regarded as 'prizes' and British crews were given monetary compensation equating to their market value from the Naval Prize Fund.

Captains and officers received a higher share than the men. The *Thetis* was carrying silver coin to the value of $1,385,292 which equated at the time to a staggering £311,690 Sterling. In addition, gold coin, cocoa and other luxury goods took the estimated total value of the cargo to £618,040, the equivalent of £54,000,000 today. This was the largest prize fund ever distributed in the history of the Royal Navy, and was divided equally among the four frigates involved.

As a lieutenant, Quilliam's share was £5,091 7s 3d, equivalent in today's terms to something like £450,000. It was this prize money, rather than simply being commissioned as an officer, which was to propel Quilliam into the ranks of the gentry in the Isle of Man, though of course it must be remembered that it was the fact that he was an officer in the first place which meant he garnered such a large share. An ordinary seaman on the *Ethalion* received a rather more modest £182, though as their annual pay was around £12 it was still the equivalent of fifteen years' wages. With success however almost came disaster, for little more than two months later *Ethalion* was wrecked on the French coast, and it would appear that Quilliam was aboard at the time. To give an idea of how reliant officers in particular were upon prize money, and how a significant capture could make a major difference to the fortunes of a family, we have a letter dated August 1800 to Robert Heywood in Douglas from Paul Crebbin of Santon, serving at sea in HMS *St Albans* on the North American Station, off Nova Scotia:

> When I wrote you last I was in full expectation of seeing you in the Island this summer but on the arrival of Sir William Parker on this station a few days ago, finding no captain of Marines on board the *St. Albans*, and the *Asia* under sailing orders for England he gave orders for my immediate removal with the greatest number of my men into the above ship where I am likely to remain at least another twelve months… but my good sir I trust and rest confident that your exertions and good attentions towards my Mother and Sisters will by no

means abate, I have the pleasure to tell you that I am now with a Captain a very active cruiser and am likely to make something handsome which should I be fortunate with my other expectations will put it fully in my power to extricate my family out of every difficulty and believe me it is sincerely the object of my heart. I shall hold myself much indebted to you to assist me in this arduous undertaking with your good council and information the best plan to go on and how to remit when I have it in my power. Such a number of small debts I think would be better drawn into a narrow focus and invested in the hands of an individual taking security on the general property, but on this you will oblige me with your advice relying firmly On your goodness in interfering in this business and in hope of soon hearing from you ... I am truly distressed by [my sister's] last letter to hear of the ill state of my Mother's health. Do my dear Sir give her every consolation in your power as I fear she injures her health by fretting from the embarrassing state of our affairs. Do write soon and address me on board of *H.M.S St. Albans*, Halifax, Nova Scotia.[76]

By contrast, for the master of a slave ship the pay though more regular was heavily dependent upon the bonuses which he might be able to claim. It was also at times a far more risky and dangerous occupation, with as well as the possibility of a slave insurrection, the constant threat from enemy privateers. Hugh Crow was now captain of the *Will*, another Liverpool ship. Earlier that year he had had a brush with the French when, near Tobago, the *Will* was attacked by a large French privateer of eighteen guns, who gave her two broadsides, and attempted to board her, but received such a destructive fire from the *Will's* guns, loaded with round shot and broken copper dross, that he sheered off. The whole action lasted several hours, but the *Will* had emerged battered yet triumphant. Despite the loss of several slaves to hits from the French, on that occasion Crow was still able to claim the £100 bounty awarded by the government. Now:

> To add to my satisfaction, Mr. Aspinall appointed a fine ship, the *Lord Stanley*, to sail with me on the next voyage. To Mr. Kirby, my mate, was given the command of that vessel, and she was placed in every respect entirely under my orders. Both ships, together with some others that were to join us, being fitted for sea, and with valuable cargoes, I received my instructions, which were of the most liberal nature, and we sailed in October, 1800, for the coast of Africa. We encountered some severe gales of wind, and did not reach Bonny till after a passage of ten weeks ... After completing our cargo, we sailed in company, all in good health, and arrived at Jamaica without losing a man. Indeed my friends at Kingston used to say 'Crow has come again, and, as usual, his whites and blacks are as plump as cotton bags.'[77]

On his return from this trip, Crow was presented with a silver tray and silver cup by Lloyd's the underwriters, in recognition of his efforts in saving his ships from the French on several occasions, and also received an additional sum of money from them.

* * *

In 1800, Prussia, Russia, Sweden and Denmark had formed the Armed Neutrality of the North to resist the British plan to prevent neutral countries trading with France. The Danish fleet was powerful and potentially of great danger, and so the British demanded that the ships be leased to them, or be destroyed. On 12 March 1801 a Royal Navy fleet sailed against Denmark under the command of Sir Hyde Parker, with Vice Admiral Lord Nelson as his deputy, to prevent the possible seizure of the Danish fleet by French forces. As they arrived off Copenhagen, negotiations with the Danes to avoid war were still ongoing. Whilst this was happening the Danes took full advantage of the delay to fortify the harbour and remove marker buoys from the approach channel. Negotiations failed, and so the British fleet passed under Kronenburg Castle and into the outer reaches of Copenhagen harbour. Nelson's plan was for the frigate squadron under Commander Riou of HMS *Amazon* to engage the Trekroner batteries, whilst the larger line of battle ships engaged the Danish fleet. Among the Manx sailors present was Lieutenant John Quilliam, also of the frigate HMS *Amazon*. Quilliam's journal for the morning of 2 April, the day of the action runs as follows:

> Moderate and cloudy. At 10, the fleet weighed in succession and bore up in a line of battle. At 10 1/2, weighed and hove to; 10 3/4, bore up and commenced firing at the enemy's floating batteries. Observed the *Bellona* and *Russell* aground on the middle ground; passed between them and the line of battle. At 11.5, anchored by the stern next ahead of the *Defiance*, Rear-Admiral Graves. At 11 1/2, the *Blanche* having anchored on our starboard beam, made the signal to her No. 4 [to take appointed station], and soon after repeated it. At noon, the enemy kept up a heavy fire, which we returned. P.m.– Light airs; the fleet keeping up a heavy fire on the shore. About 40 minutes past 12, the *Alcmene* being on our starboard beam, made the signal No. 39 [discontinue the engagement], cut her cable and stood off; she was soon followed by the *Blanche*. Observed the same signal flying on board the *London*, but we continued our fire till 1.15, when the signal being repeated by the Rear-Admiral, cut the cable and stood off. At 1.18, Captain Riou was killed by a round shot. At 2.10, anchored in 7 fathoms, Copenhagen town SW, 7 miles. At 2, a Danish flag of truce went off to the *Elephant*, when the fire ceased. Of the enemy, one floating battery blew up. Main and mizen masts

and bowsprit wounded, one of the carronades dismounted, a number of the lower shrouds and running rigging shot away.
Number: Killed, 14, and Wounded, 23.[78]

A number of myths grew up surrounding this battle. One has it that at one point things were going badly and Parker gave orders to break off the fight, at which point Nelson famously put his telescope to his blind eye, claiming not to have seen the signal, and fought on to win the day. Another famous story concerning this battle, repeated in *Manx Worthies* and elsewhere, is that Nelson visited the *Amazon* during the battle and after the death of Riou. He is supposed to have enquired who was in command, to which Quilliam answered from below decks, 'I am'. Nelson then enquired how things were going, to which Quilliam is famously supposed to have answered, 'Middlin'. However it is difficult to reconcile this story with Nelson's known movements during the action, so either the incident took place after the battle, or the enquiry actually came from Riou before he was killed, and has subsequently erroneously been attributed to Nelson.

Although the battle successfully neutralised the threat posed by the Danish fleet in the short term, British forces would before long have to return there. However, manoeuvring was also taking place at diplomatic level. The resignation of Britain's Prime Minister the hard-line William Pitt the Younger, coupled with renewed fears of war with Russia, and a widespread belief that a cessation of hostilities would bring an end to Pitt's hated income tax, led to an acceptance of French peace overtures. The Treaty of Amiens was signed on 25 March 1802, by Joseph Bonaparte and the Marquess Cornwallis as a 'Definitive Treaty of Peace'. It ended hostilities between the French Republic and Great Britain during the French Revolutionary Wars. The consequent Peace of Amiens lasted just over one year (until 18 May 1803) and was the only period of peace between 1793 and 1815. Under the treaty, Britain recognised the French Republic, the King of England gave up his claim to the throne of France, and both sides agreed to return captured territory. Both Napoleon Bonaparte and

THE FRENCH REVOLUTIONARY WARS

Pitt (who would shortly return to Downing Street) regarded the peace as a temporary one, whilst they regrouped.

The cessation of hostilities, albeit temporarily, allowed trading vessels to go about their business unmolested by enemy privateers. A letter of instruction sent in May 1802 to a Manx sea captain, Charles Kneale, by his Liverpool employers Thomas Leyland & Company, survives. In part it reads:

> Having appointed you to the command of our ship *Lottery* you are to proceed in her immediately to Bonny on the coast of Africa. We have put on board her an abundant and well assorted cargo, an invoice of which you will receive herewith, and on your arrival at Bonny you are to barter it for 290 Negroes. Besides which we expect you will be able to procure a quantity of palm oil, which you will take especial care to put into puncheons, well iron hooped, and that you will have a surplus of cargo left to bring home, which must be kept dry and preserved from damage.

The letter goes on to specify the ages and genders of slaves to be purchased, but the following paragraph states:

> In your treatment of the Negroes, show them every indulgence that will be consistent with the safety of the ship; do not suffer your officers or crew to offer the least abuse to them, take care that their provisions are cooked in that way which is most agreeable to them and to such as are sick allow every ... comfort that your ship affords.[79]

Whether or not Kneale would have taken serious regard of this instruction is debateable, but perhaps it was a sign that attitudes towards the slave trade in Britain were changing; a greater incentive for Kneale to concern himself with the welfare of the slaves comes further down the letter – the details of the commission he was to receive personally from the funds raised by their sale upon arrival at Barbados.

So ended one of the most intense periods of military activity in the history of the Isle of Man. Manx men had served afloat in a variety of capacities, willingly and unwillingly, in a protracted and drawn out campaign for control of the seas and of the trade routes. Those trade routes now were vital to the growing economies of the European powers, for it was the strength of those economies which enabled them to wage war on a previously unprecedented scale. However, whilst it would be difficult to point to a single Manx naval officer during the Seven Years' War, by the end of the Revolutionary Wars Manxmen were appearing in increasing numbers in a commissioned capacity on Royal Navy ships. When this intense state of conflict drew rather suddenly to a close, yet with the political and territorial rivalry between Britain and France still largely unresolved, only a few would have believed that this period of peace could be anything but short lived.

Chapter 5

The Napoleonic Wars

Hostilities recommenced between Britain and France after just over one year of peace. Neither side had fully adhered to the terms of the Treaty of Amiens, and the British especially had been reluctant to abandon captured colonial prizes. In particular, their failure to evacuate Malta as agreed angered Napoleon, and this alongside his avowed intention to shut Britain out of Europe (which inflamed British patriotic feeling) led to a renewed outbreak of war. This era from 1803 to 1815 is frequently referred to by historians as the Napoleonic Wars, as a form of shorthand, though in point of fact Napoleon Bonaparte would not become Emperor of France for a further two years. The dozen years which followed would witness the denouement of the naval campaign between Britain and France, with arguably the most famous naval battle in history taking place at Trafalgar.

In the Isle of Man, the herring season of 1803 was as poor as that of the previous year had been rich. The herring were late in arriving, but when they did at last appear in September, the fishermen were in such terror of the Impress Service that they did not dare put to sea. In the first week of October the boats ventured out, but not one eighth of the prepared barrels were used. In the early part of the following year the nemesis of the Manx fishermen, the Regulating Officer Captain Samuel Cable passed away and was buried in St George's churchyard. For some years Cable had been assisted in his duties by Lieutenant Joseph Clarke RN, who appears to have been the son of Captain Edward Clarke, an officer in the merchant service. The younger Clarke now took over the task of recruiting sailors and became the naval impressment officer on the Island; he was consequently much feared. He was, it seems, more efficient in this regard than his predecessor Cable, in part at least because he made use of a boat and crew hired from John Joseph Bacon, called the *Three Friends*. In November 1803 Clarke described to the Commissioners of the Admiralty:

> The very handsome manner in which Mr Bacon volunteered his vessel & men, in going round to Ramsey to secure some seamen detected there smuggling salt ... Mr Bacon's vessel was six days, very actively employed for the good of His Majesty's Service, when no charge regularly be made for it, by which exertion several good seamen were secured, and from the unremitted exertion of Mr Bacon since that time, I humbly beg their Lordships will consider the case, and direct the Honourable Commissioners of the Navy, to allow Mr Bacon payment for those six days, his vessel having been fitted up as a Tender, in the completest manner and to my perfect satisfaction.[80]

Bacon was still assisting Clarke in 1804, but on a more permanent, less ad hoc basis, as another letter testifies:

> ... he has provided an excellent Boat and Oars and fitted out the Tender much to my satisfaction, and manned with four steady good men ever ready to give me assistance. I am well convinced he has lost money by his present contract but much to his credit he has chearfully [sic] provided every necessary article wanted – the wear and tear of this vessel is very great. I therefore give it as my opinion that the £31.10.0 per month that Mr Bacon asks is not too much and that even at that rate he will not have much for his Wherry, but I conceived it my duty to make the best contract I could for the Government.[81]

Bacon's contract engaged him to provide the *Three Friends* at the service of the Regulating Officer, crewed by a master and three hands at the expense of the owner, for as long as she was required on Admiralty service. So much was the press gang feared that when in July of 1804 the Duke of Atholl arrived, bringing with him protections from impressment, which could be obtained by fishermen from the Customs House, these were greatly valued. The protections lasted for three months and were obtained upon payment of a fee. To give a sense of the scale of the Impress Service by this era, in 1805, in order to keep up the supplies of men to the navy, forty-three permanent stations or rendezvous were maintained in Great Britain and Ireland, with an establishment of twenty-seven captains and sixty-three lieutenants, permanently on duty, established ...

> ... in those parts of the United Kingdom where seamen chiefly resort, at which stations volunteers and impressed men are asked, and deserters from the Naval Service are apprehended.[82]

In Douglas, Lieutenant Joseph Clarke's Rendezvous was located at the Old Fort tavern, on Fort Street. It was common practice for inns to be utilised for this purpose, and they were frequently decorated with flags and bunting to make them conspicuous. It was also conveniently located next to Douglas Fort, the cellar of which had been used prior to the construction of the courthouse as the town lockup. It was here that the less willing recruits were held until they went onboard a tender, when they would be placed in the 'press room', a secure part of the ship under lock and key. Often this would be overcrowded, but until the men were entered upon the ship's books and rated, they were not subject to naval discipline and would almost certainly try to escape.

As to how the press gangs identified sailors (because although in extremes landsmen would be seized, experienced seamen were always preferred) this was relatively straightforward: sailors in this era were easily marked out by their hands, always covered in tar from the ropes on which they pulled to reef and unfurl sails. They had a distinctive gait, often described as bow legged, acquired from many years of maintaining their balance on a pitching deck, and their speech also set them apart, for the complex maritime terminology of the era meant that sailors spoke a language almost of their own, often quite incomprehensible to land dwellers.

However it should not be assumed that in every instance, Clarke took Manx sailors unwillingly. An interesting court case from 1806 proves the point that there were still numerous volunteers willing to offer their services to the Royal Navy. The case centred upon two apprentices from Peel who volunteered to join the navy at Douglas, and were sent to Liverpool on a ship belonging to the Impress Service. Their employer as a result sought damages from Clarke in court. The papers from the case reveal much about how the system worked:

> Philip Cowley of the Town of Douglas being sworn and examined deposeth and saith that upon the afternoon of a Sunday in the month of July last, as he best recollects as to the time [he] accompanied William Lewthwaite and two lads of the names of Crebbin and Waterson, which two lads had come to the Rendezvous for the purpose of entering as Volunteers in His Majesty's Navy, to the house of the Defendant Captain [sic] Clark. That upon that occasion the Defendant Captain Clark asked where they were from, what trade they followed, and whether they were apprentices – and the said lads informed the Defendant that they followed no trade, but going to the fishing, and that they were not apprentices. That the said two lads then entered with the Defendant to serve in His Majesty's Navy, and received a shilling a piece. That from the time of their so entering into the said Service to the time of the sailing of the Tender, the said two lads were not confined, but were at liberty to go about the Town as they chose. That the Deponent belongs to the Press Gang and the Deponent with they of the Gang have general orders from the Defendant not to impress apprentices wither by Sea or Land.

THE NAPOLEONIC WARS

Edward Gell of Castletown, a constable, was in possession of a warrant obtained by the employer from Deemster Lace, ordering the release of the apprentices. According to his testimony on the day he travelled to Douglas to serve the warrant, he visited both the Rendezvous and the house of Joseph Clarke, only to be met with obfuscation from Lewthwaite and another member of the press gang, Edward Creer, both of whom refused to reveal the whereabouts of Clarke. Cowley meanwhile stated that he had seen Gell on the quay whilst he was on the tender with the recruits, but,

> At that time [he] did not understand that the said lads were apprentices, nor did he know that they were until some time after the Tender had sailed, when the lads informed [him] upon the Passage that they were apprentices and that they would rather throw themselves overboard than go back to their master.[83]

The case against Clarke was dismissed. Lewthwaite, Creer and Cowley were probably midshipmen. Sometimes additional help was received from the military forces of the Island. On one occasion a corporal and three privates of the Manx Yeomanry Cavalry spent a day and a night in:

> Assisting Lieutenant Clarke, [and a] Midshipman, in apprehending and bringing to gaol a secreted seaman, and next day escorting him to rendezvous, Douglas, a distance of 16 miles.

Later no less than three such detachments were on duty assisting the midshipmen to find deserters from the Royal Navy, and at the end of the month a party under a sergeant comprising up to eight rank and file assisted the press gang in: 'Apprehending some smugglers and proper persons to serve in the Navy'.[84]

Impressment was also used as a punishment by the civil power. One account records the fact that Deemster John Crellin ordered that Thomas

Cowley, a hatter of Ballaugh, whom he described as a 'vagabond and a nuisance to Society' be handed over to Lieutenant Clarke for impressment into the Royal Navy at the Rendezvous in Douglas. By some means however, Cowley managed to have himself arrested for debt before this could happen. He was then confined in Castle Rushen, from which he could not be extracted.

Later the new Lieutenant Governor, Cornelius Smelt, also tried to have those engaged in the herring fishery to be exempt from impressment, and applied to the Home Secretary Lord Hawkesbury for this purpose. Smelt duly received a reply, which was widely circulated in the Island, stating that:

> Instructions have been given to his Majesty's Ships, not to Impress Persons concerned in the Herring Fishery; and any men who appear to have been impressed from this Occupation will be released.[85]

Despite this, Joseph Clarke remained greatly feared, and Manx fishermen and sailors continued for some years after to live in terror of being impressed. After Clarke died, and was buried at Braddan churchyard, it appears that the Rendezvous was closed and there was no Regulating Officer permanently in Douglas.

* * *

On 21 October 1805 perhaps the most famous sea battle in history was fought off the coast of Spain, between the British fleet under Admiral Lord Nelson on the one hand, and a combined Franco-Spanish fleet on the other. Nelson's plan was brilliantly simple. Dividing his force into two columns, they sailed towards the ragged enemy line. Although the leading vessels of the two columns suffered the full weight of hostile fire for more than ten minutes, Nelson had rightly counted upon their gunnery being poor. As the fleets closed, the superior shooting of the Royal Navy wrought havoc in the French and Spanish ships.

THE NAPOLEONIC WARS

Yet for whatever it did achieve, the Battle of Trafalgar, despite all that has been claimed for it in the intervening years, did not in itself prevent Napoleon from invading Britain. The Emperor had already gone cold on this idea, and as the battle was being fought at Trafalgar his army had long since left its invasion camps around Boulogne and was fighting against the Austrians at Ulm. Napoleon had never really understood (or valued) sea power, being a soldier through and through. The real significance of the battle was that it severely weakened French naval strength, and meant at least that France could not seriously challenge the British at sea again. This left Britain effectively in control of the world's oceans, a position in which it would remain until a new threat emerged in 1914.

The most famous Manx participant in the Battle of Trafalgar was Lieutenant John Quilliam of HMS *Victory*. Quilliam was living proof of the meritocratic nature of the Georgian navy. Unlike the army, in which position and authority could be purchased by those with money, the navy was considered too important to national defence, and here what counted was skill and ability. Quilliam had joined the navy as a volunteer, and worked his way up the promotion ladder to commissioned rank. We catch a glimpse of him at the start of the battle. He was watching another ship as she went into action, and saw her break the enemy's line, as we are told by a midshipman on board the *Victory*, George Westphal:

> I had left my quarters to make a report to Quilliam, our First-Lieutenant, who was standing near Lord Nelson on the quarter-deck, watching the *Belleisle*. Every person thought she would have opened her fire long before she did, the enemy having been firing at her, and, indeed, having visibly damaged her spars some time previously. But the *Belleisle* still preserved her fire until she had brought both broadsides, as it appeared to us in the *Victory*, to bear on the ships on each side of her. She was within pistol-shot when her two broadsides were discharged simultaneously and with the precision of a volley of musketry; upon seeing which, Lord Nelson exclaimed, 'Nobly done, Hargood !'[86]

The best known story concerning Quilliam has it that at Trafalgar, when the wheel of the *Victory* was carried away by an enemy cannon ball, he went below and organised a jury rig, a temporary method of controlling the rudder by means of ropes. This vital knowledge of how a ship worked would have been born of many years of experience at sea, and it proved essential at the height of the battle in allowing *Victory* to close with the French ship *Bucentaure*. Quilliam himself wrote in his own log of the events of the battle as he saw them:

> **About 1:15** Admiral the Right Honorable Lord Nelson K.B.etc and Commander in Chief, was wounded in the Shoulder. At 1:30 The *Redoutable*, having struck her colors we ceased firing our starboard Guns, but continued engaged with the *Santisima Trinidador* and some of the Enemies Line on the starboard side.
>
> Observed the *Temeraire* between the *Redoutable* and another French Ship of the Line, both of which had struck. The action continuing general until 3 o'clock, when several of the Enemy's ships around us had struck, observed the *Royal Sovereign* with the top of her main and mizzen masts and several of the enemy ships around her dis-masted.
>
> **At 3.30** observed 4 sail of the Enemy's Van Tack, and stand along our weather line to windward, fired our Larboard guns at those they would reach.
>
> **At 3:40** made the signal, for our ships to keep their wind and engage the Enemy's Van coming along our weather line.
>
> **At 4:15** the Spanish Rear Admiral to windward struck to some ships, which had tacked after them, observed one of the Enemy's Ships blow up, and 14 sail standing towards Cadiz, and 3 standing to the Southward, partial firing occured until 3:40 when a Victory having been reported to the Admiral Right

THE NAPOLEONIC WARS

Honorable Lord Nelson K.B.etc and Honored Commander in Chief, he died of his wounds.

At 5 the mizen mast all about 10 feet above the Poop the lower masts, yards and bowsprit all crippled, rigging and sails very much cut, the Ships around us very much crippled, several of our ships pursuing the enemy to Leeward, saw Vice Admiral Collingwood's Flag Flying on board HMS *Euruyalus*, and some of our ships taking possession of the Prizes. Struck top Gt. Masts got up runners, and tackles, to secure the masts employed clearing the wreck of the yards and rigging, wore ship and sounded in 32 fms sandy bottom, stood to the southward under the remnants of Foresail and maintopsail, sounded from 13-19 fms.[87]

Strangely, Quilliam himself makes no mention of the incident with the jury rig, nor is it recorded in the ship's log as one might expect. It did however appear in print for the first time not long after the battle, and before the myth-making around Quilliam had really begun, so it may well be true, and certainly Quilliam never denied it. A number of other Manxmen – officers and ratings – also served at Trafalgar.

Some sixty-six sailors and three marines of Manx birth are believed to have fought at the battle. Just a few examples stand for many; Hugh Bainbridge was born in Peel, the son of James Bainbridge and Ellinor nee Shimmin. He was on board HMS *Leviathan* at Trafalgar as Able Seaman. He had his right arm shattered by a cannon shot during the battle and had the limb amputated beneath the shoulder joint. He was treated at Plymouth Hospital, before being invalided out of the Navy. He received £40 from the Lloyd's Patriotic Fund for Wounds. David Christian was born on the Isle of Man in 1779. He was on board HMS *Africa* at Trafalgar as a Private in the Royal Marines. He also was wounded at the battle, and lost his left arm below the elbow. He received £40 from Lloyd's Patriotic Fund for Wounds. He was invalided out of the service in 1806.

MANXMEN AT SEA IN THE AGE OF NELSON, 1760–1815

The most detailed biography of an ordinary Manx sailor at Trafalgar is that of John Lawson, of HMS *Revenge*. He was born in Andreas around 1774, the illegitimate son of Joaney Moore. Her father had turned her out of his house on account of her 'mishap', and she brought the boy up alone. Around the age of 14, he was apprenticed on a merchant vessel. At some point he had been taken by a press gang, and served a number of years in the Far East, eventually returning to Britain aboard HMS *Centurion*. He was subsequently involved in the Spithead mutiny of 1797, being one of the leaders of the men who went on strike for better conditions in the navy. When the Peace of Amiens brought the Revolutionary Wars to a close, he returned home to the Isle of Man, where his mother at first did not recognise him. When he had left, he spoke no English, only Manx. When he returned, he could only speak English. With the outbreak of hostilities once more he returned to the Royal Navy as a volunteer, serving at Trafalgar. Afterwards, he was one of the prize crews put aboard a captured ship, and was drowned when it foundered in the storm which followed the battle.

Perhaps the saddest story is that of Lieutenant Robert Benjamin Young, by now captain of the *Entreprenante*, one of the smallest ships involved in the fighting at Trafalgar. The day before the battle he received directions from Lord Nelson (who had known him for some years beforehand) to keep close to his flag-ship, as it was Nelson's intention to send him home with the news of the victory which he anticipated. Towards the close of the action Young was able to save as many as 168 of the crew of the French 74-gun ship *Achille*, which had caught fire and which blew up an hour later. During the tremendous gale that ensued, although crowded with prisoners and suffering from a shortage of drinking water, he was tireless in ascertaining, and in correctly reporting, the position of the captured prizes. One of these, the 74-gun Spanish vessel *Bahama*, whose crew had overpowered their guard, would have succeeded in making her escape into Cádiz, had Young not prevented it by signalling what was happening. The prize crew from the *Bahama* were taken on board his vessel, and Young distributed food and clothing both to them and the French crew rescued earlier.

THE NAPOLEONIC WARS

Notwithstanding that it had been arranged that he was to carry home the despatches recounting the victory, to his dismay Young was sent instead with the duplicates of them to Faro in Portugal; through this he lost both the promotion and the financial reward that traditionally went to bearers of good news. The only reward he received for his services at Trafalgar, was a sword from the Patriotic Society. Young remained bitter about his treatment for the remainder of his life. Despite his bravery, he lacked the connections which were also necessary to advance his career, and the highest rank which he achieved was that of commander.

Quilliam did not accompany the *Victory* back to home waters, instead remaining at Gibraltar to repair and refit other vessels, but when after a journey of five weeks the battered flagship finally made it into the English Channel, a Manx eyewitness caught sight of her. Lieutenant Edward Christian of Lewaigue, serving with the 43rd Light Infantry and writing from Shorncliffe Camp near Folkestone to his uncle, told him that:

> The *Victory* with the body of Lord Nelson on board is now anchored off this cliff, but the sea runs so high that no boat will put off. She is a grand wreck.[88]

The death of Nelson at Trafalgar caused a nationwide outpouring of grief. There was also tremendous pride felt in the Isle of Man (as elsewhere) in Nelson's crushing victory over the French and Spanish.

* * *

By the early part of the Napoleonic Wars, the threat of privateers in the Irish Sea had subsided, and following Trafalgar the main theatre of operations for the British was the West Indies. The trafficking of slaves continued against the backdrop of the wars, and although Britain would soon abolish the trade, slavery was an integral part of what the conflict was about. Both Britain and France derived great wealth from their plantations, particularly those producing sugar, and for this, slaves were essential. The warships of both sides were frequently employed in protecting this commerce at sea, or indeed, in attempting to interrupt that commerce. As a letter from a Manx mariner, Joseph Clarke's father Captain Edward Clarke, to the owners of his ship *Rein Deer*, describes. It was later published in the *Liverpool Chronicle*. Dated Kingston, Jamaica 31 December 1805, it tells of an encounter with a heavily armed French schooner privateer out of St Domingo, within twenty-four hours' sail of the Jamaican capital:

> After a constant fire for an hour and a half within pistol shot, from our great guns and musquetry, we had the pleasure of seeing his fore and main-top masts and top-sails come tumbling down, and otherwise much disabled; the enemy being thus crippled, formed the desperate resolution of grapling, hoisting his bloody flag, which was immediately answered by the *Rein Deer* hoisting hers also.
>
> He succeeded in lashing himself with regular stoppers to our fore and main-chains, conceiving our guns were of a length under which he might lay secure, while he attempted to carry [capture] the ship sword in hand, by his very superior numbers. Perceiving his intention, we had just time to prepare him a bill of fare; our twelve pounds carronades were filled with cannister shot, and so nicely pointed downwards, that their effect was tremendous.
>
> His dexterity in getting discharged from such a reception was so great, that several of his crew were left in our chains, and jumped overboard, but very few of them reached the vessel. Our running rigging and braces being shot away, alone prevented our bringing him in; he took to his sweeps, and got out of our reach as fast as possible.
>
> I cannot speak too highly of Mr. Howard, my first mate, and all my officers and men. Their steady and determined bravery displayed an honourable consciousness of their own credit, and of their duty towards the Owners and Underwriters, in

the protection of a property placed in their hands. The slaves that I had taught on the passage the use of musquetry behaved extremely well, and did the enemy much mischief.

I am, however, extremely sorry to report the unavoidable consequence attendant to such obstinate occurrences. We had two men killed, and six wounded, mostly badly, with two slaves slightly. I have been unfortunate in having my right arm shattered most severely by a piece of iron, two inches long and an inch broad, which has been taken from it, and, untill within these few days, the amputating knife continued suspended. I thank God for a favourable change. At the same instant I had my arm shattered, the trumpet was knocked from my other in the act of bringing her broadside to bear.[89]

Here again is evidence of the arming of some of the slaves to fight the French, but the successful defence of the ship is all the more remarkable when one considers that half the slaver's crew had previously been taken off by the Royal Navy. Worse treatment was meted out to Hugh Crow on a voyage in the same waters that year. This time he was captain of the *Mary* of Liverpool, near Tobago when he ran across two cruisers which he took to be French privateers. After putting up a desperate fight of some seven hours, in which he was wounded and several of the crew and slaves were killed, as he prepared to surrender he discovered to his dismay that the two opposing ships were actually the British sloops HMS *Dart* and *Wolverine*. After the discovery of the mistake, both ships provided help in dealing with the wounded, and the crew of the *Mary* were given exemptions from impressment as a form of compensation. Public opinion in Britain however had been turning against the African Trade for some years, and now William Wilberforce and his supporters had succeeded in having it outlawed in the British Empire. The following year, Crow would command what was probably the last legal slave crossing, having been specially chosen to take charge of the slave ship *Kitty's Amelia*.

In the West Indies however life at sea was dangerous enough on its own. Weather forecasting was little understood, and this region was prone to devastating hurricanes. As an indicator of just how unpredictable these waters could be, we have the example of Philip Crebbin of Santon, who met his fate not at the hands of the enemy, but the weather. Lieutenant Edward Burt the commander of his ship HMS *Redbridge* wrote:

> It is with sorrow I am called upon to be the person to communicate the bad news of the loss you sustain by the loss of your brother. He was on the schooner I've the honor to command, as mate and was placed with me when the *Vanguard* sailed for England for the attainment of promotion and being sent on board his Majesty's late ship in order to identify deserters and when parted from me a tremendous squall upset her and the poor fellow with 100 of the crew went down with her. According to the established regulations of the Navy his effects were sold amongst those on board of his rank and I have reserved £10 to pay a bill of his on the North side of Jamaica, and in his ticket lodged in the Navy Office he has due £11.0.1 where on application you will be able to receive his pay for the *Redbridge* and *Vanguard* for which he has due a good deal of pay. His letters I have destroyed as it appears most satisfactory and if I can by any means serve you concerning any question you may require I shall be glad...[90]

The schooner *Redbridge* went down on 4 November 1806, off New Providence Island (now known as Nassau in the Bahamas). She was a former French vessel captured a year earlier in the West Indies, and the Royal Navy was generally wary of schooners such as this, which carried too much sail on top and were apt to capsize in high winds. Often they would cut down the spars to a shorter length if a ship like this was taken into the Royal Navy, in order to make it more stable, but perhaps it did not happen in this case.

THE NAPOLEONIC WARS

By now, the name of John Quilliam and his exploits in the Royal Navy were widely known on the Isle of Man, as evidenced by the fact that the *Manks Advertiser* of 16 August 1806 carried a report of his return to the island, along with another Manx maritime hero:

> Upward of 70 passengers, it is said, arrived here in the *Duke of Atholl* (Liverpool trader) on Tuesday (12th Aug.) among whom were Captain Quilliam and Capt. Edward Clark; – the former, it is hardly necessary to say, was Lieutenant on board of the *Victory* in the ever-memorable action off Trafalgar;– he possessed the friendship and esteem of his gallant commander – Lord Nelson – and has since been promoted to the rank of Post Captain.[91]

Quilliam was on the Island for only a matter of months, for in early 1807 he was writing to the Admiralty from an address in Great Russell Street, London, but it must have been at this time that he was approached to become a member of the self-selecting House of Keys. In September 1807 he was elected by the existing members to fill a vacancy in their number, and his appointment was approved by the Governor. Perhaps more significant than his naval achievements in their eyes was the fact that Quilliam had become a landowner – much of his prize money was invested in property and his rise to join the landed elite was a testament to the social mobility which the Royal Navy offered to those of skill and ability, no matter how humble their birth.

Around this time however Quilliam also became involved in a minor scandal, for he was summoned to appear before a church court in Douglas after being named as the father of an illegitimate child. Quilliam did not attend the court, and was cited for contempt but matters were taken no further, possibly because in the meantime the baby had died. The mother, Elizabeth Gelling, would go on to appear twice more in chapter courts seeking to 'affiliate' two other men as fathers of subsequent illegitimate children. Perhaps her claim was false and she simply saw Quilliam as a wealthy man and an easy target, but the mother recorded him as the father in the church register. Interestingly, the little boy whom she had also named 'John Quilliam' was baptised at St Matthews, Douglas on 8 May 1808, some nine months after his probable return to the Island for election to the Keys.

For the British, political as well as military means were vital in containing Napoleon's ambitions and diplomacy played an important role in maintaining the various coalitions which were assembled against the French. Since the Battle of the Nile, Britain had been on cordial terms with the Ottoman Empire, but by 1806 French efforts to woo the Sultan Selim III into fresh hostilities against Russia meant that relations began to deteriorate. The British offered the Ottomans an ultimatum to expel the French ambassador, or face war. This was rejected, but Britain was too weak militarily to engage the Sultan's forces on land. Instead, Admiral Collingwood dispatched a force under Admiral Duckworth from the Mediterranean Fleet, with the intention of destroying the Ottoman navy at Constantinople. There was a disaster before the British force even entered the Dardanelles however, when HMS *Ajax* caught fire. The blaze began after the purser and his assistant (who was supposedly drunk) had negligently left a light burning in the bread room, and the ship ran aground and was destroyed on the island of Tenedos. A near contemporary account records that:

> ... a melancholy accident befell the *Ajax*, one of the ships of Sir John Duckworth's squadron. At 9 P.M., just as Captain Blackwood had retired to rest, the officer of the watch ran into the cabin and acquainted him that there was a great alarm of fire in the after part of the ship. Signals of distress were immediately made and enforced by guns. The fire had broken out in the after cockpit, and in the course of 10 minutes, notwithstanding every attempt to stifle it, the smoke became so dense, that, although the moon shone bright, the officers and men on the upper deck could only

distinguish each other by speaking or feeling; all attempts, therefore, to hoist out the boats, except the jollyboat, were ineffectual. The flames then burst up the main hatchway, thereby dividing the fore from the after part of the ship; and with the greatest difficulty, the captain, and about 381 of the officers, seamen, and marines of the ship, effected their escape, chiefly by jumping overboard from the bowsprit, or dropping into the few boats that were enabled to approach in time to be useful.[92]

More than half the crew were saved, but among the dead was James Kewley of Douglas, a Bosun's Mate. Kewley had previously served aboard the *Ajax* at the Battle of Trafalgar, and is recorded in the ship's musters as having been a volunteer. Large numbers of survivors were picked up by other British vessels in the fleet, including her captain Henry Blackwood who had been in the water clinging to an oar for an hour. Other survivors included a woman, Mrs Dunford the wife of the Acting Boatswain, and this and the fact that an infant (who sadly could not be saved) was also recovered from the water indicates that the interior of a warship in this era was far from an all-male world. Two other men who were saved from the water, Cornelius Loney and John Crane, may also have been Manx.

On 19 February 1807 the remainder of Duckworth's fleet began to force the Dardanelles, coming under fire from Ottoman shore batteries as they did so. Present here was 16-year-old Michael Finch Cosnahan, the son of John Cosnahan the High Bailiff of Douglas. Cosnahan was a First Class Volunteer aboard HMS *Pompée*, a French-built 74-gun third rate ship, which had been taken as a prize shortly after construction and thus spent almost her entire career in British service. Cosnahan had an older brother, Hugh Cosnahan, who was already on his way towards commissioned rank in the Royal Navy (he passed for lieutenant in 1813) so the family clearly had connections within the naval world. The younger Cosnahan had been aboard *Pompée* two years learning the craft of seamanship by this point, but this was probably his first real taste of combat as the shore forts opened fire and the British warships returned the same. In some cases, marines were landed to destroy the guns, and some Ottoman warships were engaged and sunk, but the majority of the Sultan's fleet withdrew out of range. Overall, the operation was a failure, but Britain continued to manoeuvre politically and diplomatically in order to form alliances against France.

As with the Sultan, where persuasion would not work, force was employed. Despite the defeat and loss of many ships in the first Battle of Copenhagen in 1801, Denmark-Norway, possessing Schleswig-Holstein and Iceland, still maintained a considerable navy. The majority of the Danish army, under the Crown Prince, was at this time defending the southern border against possible attack from the French. There was concern in Britain that Napoleon might try to force Denmark to close the Baltic Sea to British ships, perhaps by marching French troops into Zealand. The British believed that access to the Baltic was vitally important for trade as well as a major source of the necessary raw materials for building and maintaining warships, and that it gave the Royal Navy access to help Britain's allies Sweden and Russia against France. This was particularly important because for most of the Napoleonic Wars Britain was short of food and relied heavily upon imports, especially grain. The Baltic coast and the Gulf of Finland were important sources of this commodity, and it was vital that Britain kept this seaway open for trade, in spite of the hostility of the Danes. Yet after Prussia had been defeated in December 1806, the British believed Denmark's independence looked increasingly under threat from France.

On 21 January 1807, Lord Hawkesbury told the House of Lords that he had received information from someone on the Continent 'that there were secret engagements in the Treaty of Tilsit to employ the navies of Denmark and Portugal against this country'. He refused to publish the source because he said it would endanger their lives. The reports of French diplomats and merchants in northern Europe made the British government uneasy, and by mid-July the British believed that the French intended to invade Holstein in order to use Denmark against Britain. Some reports suggested that the Danes had secretly agreed to this. The possibility of the Danes closing off British access to the Baltic was now serious, and the Cabinet decided to act; a combined military and naval force was despatched, in order to capture the remainder of the Danish fleet at Copenhagen.

Again, Manx soldiers and sailors were involved. One, Lieutenant Edward Christian, wrote to his uncle from Boarup in Zealand, 18 miles west of Copenhagen, on 2 September 1807. Edward's cousin, Evan Christian, was a midshipman in the Royal Navy and served at the same action. However it was not possible for the two to meet, although Edward was able to send a message via a brother officer:

> It was not till the day previous to our landing that I heard of Evan's being in this fleet, and that by the merest accident. A company of our regiment was sent on board of the *Brunswick* for the purpose of using her boats upon debarkation, and I then heard of Evan, and immediately wrote to him, but in our hurried state I had to lament the utter impossibility of seeing him. He dined in the captain's cabin with our officers; is well; looking handsome; and is destined to serve with the Marine and Seamen Brigade. Should we both survive the conflict we shall have a happy meeting. He is much liked on board, and is attentive to his duty. I long to see him. The fleet has remained hitherto inactive, unable to pass the Crown batteries.

Edward Christian's next letter, sent from Colchester Barracks in July 1808, refers to the death of his aunt Anne Christian, Evan's mother, on the Isle of Man. It is clear that the news had not yet reached Evan, who was still serving aboard HMS *Brunswick* in the Baltic. Another interesting aspect of this letter is Edward Christian's intention to contact John Quilliam in an attempt to have him take Evan Christian under his wing. Such was the manner in which the Royal Navy worked in this age, and family connections like this counted for a great deal.

> Aweful [sic] reports during the last month prepared me to meet that dire event which my mother's letter announced, and imparted to my mind the most acute anguish. Painfully alive are my feelings to the consequent grief of my poor cousins whose irreparable loss I most sincerely participate. In this gloom I must bring your attention to the situation of poor Evan, and measures absolutely necessary to be pursued for securing his comfort and credit in the service; and in, the first instance I strongly recommend your placing his yearly allowance each year in the hands of Mr Drinkwater, of Liverpool, who I am persuaded would take that trouble. This arrangement will prevent Evan the uncertainty and inconvenience of negotiating a draft upon the Island, which would be always objectionable in England from the remoteness of the situation and its uncertain intercourse.
>
> You will have been informed that I wrote to Evan soon after my return from the Island in consequence of my having discovered by the papers that his ship was on the point of sailing from Plymouth for some foreign station, and fearing that he might be in want of pecuniary aid and not likely to receive any in time from home, I gave him permission to draw upon me for a sum necessary for his outfit. His spirit is noble and high, and by a letter of his to his ever-to-be-lamented mother, I was grieved to find that it had been wounded by the want of pecuniary assistance. . . A short time since I had an opportunity of writing to him by a friend of mine, who is going out to Gothenburg in Sweden, the present station of the *Brunswick*; and I shall have by this post the painful task of communicating to him the mournful event.

THE NAPOLEONIC WARS

I have lately been informed of Captain Quilliam's appointment to the *Spencer* of 74 guns, and I should have much satisfaction in his taking Evan on board. I am writing to Capt Q. in favour of the son of Lady Napier, who is a midshipman under his command, and I shall take the opportunity of naming Evan to him.[93]

Such connections however were only available to those of certain classes, and for the lower orders, the welfare of family members was far more of a problem.

* * *

The prisoners in France were among those who fared the worst during the Napoleonic Wars, although it must be said that by this time, conditions had improved a little on those endured by Hugh Crow and others during the fanatical fervour which immediately followed the French Revolution. Bonaparte himself took an interest in the welfare of prisoners of war, and recognised that they were entirely dependent upon the largess of the capturing power. Of all the prisoners in France, the British were probably treated best, with the cruellest and harshest treatment meted out to the Spanish. Even for the British however conditions were largely dependent upon class, and whilst officers were usually given a certain amount of freedom, those in the ranks were often held in damp dungeons.

By this stage in the war a number of Manxmen were in French hands, and money was sometimes raised in parish churches for their benefit. Alexander Crigan, a son of Bishop Crigan, had qualified in medicine and wishing to see something of the world had taken a position as surgeon aboard a British warship. His vessel however was wrecked on the French coast, and he along with the rest of the crew were taken prisoner. He was moved from prison to prison but managed to get a letter sent home from Arras, where he was then incarcerated. Part of it read:

> ... soon after my arrival here I forwarded a petition to you my dear father requesting you would send a copy to the Governor of the Island from the few Manks men at this depot (all in fact who are in France) ... The petition merely requested you to lay their situation before their countrymen in the most Pathetic manner & beg some pecuniary assistance for them; this kind of assistance has been granted by all the Towns of the United Kingdom to the seamen prisoners in France who belonged formerly to them (extra to the Patriotic Fund) should any money be thus procured, by sending it to my agent he will lodge me credit in France for it, and I through him can forward you the receipts from the men here. In the mean time I have done all in my power for them. Cain I have got into my house as a servant, and besides shirts etc I divide my French pay among the others – this is but little, but little with them (as they are situated) is of great importance.[94]

A few years later a similar letter acknowledging help for local prisoners in France reached the Isle of Man from Thomas Crellin, of Peel, then a captive at Longwy. Addressed to Robert Cannell, of Douglas, it runs as follows:

> Dear friend, Your favour of the 11th of June came to hand, also a remittance of £40, for which I received 661 livres 8 sols. I wrote to the different depots, and find there are 27 of our countrymen, among whom I impartially distributed [the money]. The following are the names of the prisoners: At Cambray – John Lace, Onchan; Thomas Farragher, Peel; Thomas Kermode, Port St. Mary; Robert Quaye, Maughold; Robert Kelly Braddan; Robert Kail, Ramsey. At Givet – Ross McKissack Castletown; Robert Creer, Castletown; Wm. Garrett, Douglas; Wm. Benally, Foxdale. At Verdon [sic] – Daniel Clarke, Peel; John Clague, Douglas. At Besancon –

> Thomas Radcliffe, John Parr Whittam, Wm. Johnston, John Corlett, all of Douglas; Thomas Taubman, Castletown; Thomas Cannell, Peel; Edward Moore, Andreas. At Longwy – Thomas Cummins, Castletown; Patrick Kewley, Ballaugh; Michael Cowin, Peel; Robert Quayle, Ballasalla; Thomas Crellin, Peel. At Arras – Wm. Kegg, Castletown. At Sarra Louis [sic] - Thomas Clucas, Marown. There is another, John Lace of Ramsey, not yet found.[95]

Of these Thomas Faragher, of Peel, was captured in 1809; Thomas Cannell (son of Robert, of Peel) had been captured in September 1805, when the convoy escort ship HMS *Calcutta* had been drawn into an action with a French squadron in the English Channel; Michael Cowin (son of Thomas, of Peel) was a sailor on the *Sophia* when captured in 1804; Thomas Crellin, the writer of the letter, was on the ship *Hamilton*, captured in 1806. Eventually, most of them found their way back to the Island.

* * *

The ongoing infringement by both sides of the rights of American citizens on the high seas led President Jefferson, in protest, to impose an embargo on exports both to the French and to Great Britain. Nevertheless there were frequent breaches of the embargo in the Bay of Fundy, close to Maine in the United States, and a thriving smuggling trade grew up in Passamaquoddy Bay, through which thousands of barrels of US flour were illegally imported into British territory. Despite the peace which had existed between Britain and the United States since the end of the Revolutionary War, there was still much tension between the two, particularly in the border area of New Brunswick, in modern Canada. Since the independence of the United States, the region around Campobello and Passamaquoddy Bay had been problematic for both the officers of the Halifax squadron and for colonial officials. The boundaries between New Brunswick and Maine were imprecisely defined and disputed, and the customs officers on both sides of the frontier were prone to cooperation with smugglers and deserters from the British Navy and Army.

Manx naval officer Lieutenant William Frissell was in command of the gunboat HMS *Plumper*, a brig designed for speed which, though built by the British, incorporated many features of the fast American schooners of this era. She was employed in patrolling the bay and policing imports from the United States. It was work not wholly dissimilar to that of the revenue service around the Isle of Man, except that here the inhabitants and local customs officers on both sides of the border were in connivance, making the Royal Navy deeply unpopular. On 17 May 1808, William Frissell wrote to the Admiralty from Saint Andrews, on Passamaquoddy Bay, which was bisected by the Maine/New Brunswick border, in the following terms:

> ... the conduct of the inhabitants of late has been very improper in the conducting the Flour from the opposite side, by using Force, and arming boats with Harpoons or Instruments similar by which several custom house officers have been wounded.[96]

At the same time, a Royal Navy officer named Flintoph had come in for sharp criticism from the local population for his heavy handed approach, which included firing his guns indiscriminately, and impressing or beating up local sailors. Frissell observed in his letter that he was sorry to report that the very people who disapproved of Flintoph's conduct were acting so improperly themselves, and asked permission to impress any man involved in violent acts, in order to keep a good understanding with US officials. For the next couple of months Frissell was on convoy duty escorting supply ships bound for the West Indies from Marvel Island as far as Cape Sable. However the arrival of a powerful American vessel in these waters was a cause for some disquiet. Frissell's superior Jonathan Shortland, aboard HMS *Squirrel* at Campobello, wrote to Sir J.B. Warren on 3 September 1808:

> The *Plumper* Gun brig has this moment returned from Digby ½ pt. 6 p.m. and in consequence of the United States Frigate *Chesapeake* having arrived in Passamaquoddy Bay this day, I have again directed Lt. Frissell to put to Sea forthwith and proceed without loss of time to Digby and to request of the Post Master at Digby to forward my letter by the first safe opportunity that may occur before that post day. I did not conceive it necessary to send this letter express, on account of the heavy expense, & there being every appearance of friendship subsisting between us and the Americans in this Port; the *Chesapeake* is from a Month's cruise along the coast, she was forced to anchor in harbor de Lute, Campobello, on account of the Ebb, & light airs, consequently I sent my first Lieutenant on board her who was treated with every attention & civility, she got under way this Evening and anchored near Moose Island: I have delivered Lieut. Frissell his Press Warrant, and have directed him to after landing my letter at Digby to proceed to St. John's [sic] to procure seamen: when I clearly understand the motive of the *Chesapeake*'s appearance here, I shall send an Officer of the Impress Service to St. Andrews should anything of consequence occur I shall send a dispatch without loss of time.[97]

This incident followed hard on the heels of another in which HMS *Leopard* had made an unprovoked attack on USS *Chesapeake* off the Virginia coast that summer, which had caused outrage in the United States. In August 1809, Lieutenant William Frissell (still commanding the gunboat HMS *Plumper)* impressed a man named George Laighton from the schooner *Fairplay* as it lay in Saint John Harbour, New Brunswick. Laighton was an American, and thus managed to sue for release, though this ploy was not always successful. The ongoing Anglo-American tensions over impressment would erupt into war before long.

The ongoing war with the French however was costing the British exchequer dearly; a major source of revenue to pay for this conflict was tax on sugar from the Caribbean slave islands. With the remnants of the French fleet now largely bottled up in its harbours, the Royal Navy was largely free to conduct operations in the West Indies. However Martinique, and nearby Guadeloupe, were still a major threat to British trade in the area, providing sheltered bases from which French privateers and warships could raid British shipping, and disrupt the trade routes that were vital for the British economy. Following the Spanish alliance with Britain, the Admiralty decided to order a British squadron to neutralise the threat, beginning with Martinique. Senhouse Wilson, son of the Manx Receiver General of the same name, was appointed as a Lieutenant of HMS *Belleisle* around this time. She was part of a fleet which took part in the seizure of the Danish West Indies, following the capitulation of Copenhagen. Later Wilson took part in the capture of Martinique.

The British, as they had done previously in the American Revolutionary War, made widespread use of the convoy system to try to protect their merchant ships from harassment by the French. John Quilliam, a steady and reliable commander with excellent skills of seamanship, would prove himself one of the best convoy commanders in the Royal Navy. It was a hard job, with little glamour or glory attached to it, but Quilliam proved his worth time and again in escorting convoys into the Baltic, and later to the West Indies and back. The system was not always foolproof, for Quilliam, by this time in command of HMS *Alexandria*, wrote to the Admiralty from the Nore in June 1810:

> I beg leave to acquaint you ... That in addition to the enclosed Log of the proceedings of His Majesty's Ship under my command, that it was impossible to fill up the two last columns of the Convoy List owing to the want of materials for making their distinguishing names. I beg leave likewise to acquaint you for their Lordships' information that the total Disregards paid to the Signals by the Convoy (The English and Americans excepted) not withstanding every exertion of mine

to keep them collected all but about Seventy Sail intentionally separated during the night and in thick weather, before we made the English Lanes.[98]

In a subsequent letter, Quilliam wrote to the Admiralty asking for carronades to be substitute for some of the long guns which were presently on the Quarterdeck of the *Alexandria*. Quilliam seems to have had great faith in these weapons, as in an earlier letter he had requested two smaller versions for use in the *Alexandria*'s boats. Subsequently Quilliam was posted to command the *Crescent*, and yet again we find him in January 1811 writing to the Admiralty from Woolwich to ask for the vessel to be supplied with two 32 pounder carronades in lieu of two 9 pounder guns on the Forecastle.

The *Crescent* was on the North Sea Station and was involved in a number of skirmishes with the French around this time. In one of them her Lieutenant, Thomas Crane was injured, losing a big toe, and was temporarily invalided home. Crane was also a Manxman and a friend of Quilliam's, having previously served with him aboard the *Neptune*. One of his brothers was John Crane, who had been a sailmaker on the *Lion* on the voyage to China with Quilliam, and another brother James would later marry Quilliam's sister Elizabeth. This is not only a good illustration of the way in which naval families were closely connected in this era, but further demonstrates the fact that since the closing off of smuggling as a career option in the 1760s and 1770s, and the winding down of the slave trade in the early years of the nineteenth century, Manxmen with seafaring skills were increasingly turning to the Royal Navy to make their living.

Quilliam's near contemporary, Lieutenant William Kelly was another case in point. At this time he was aboard HMS *Illustrious*, and at the end of 1810 she was involved in the capture of Ile de France (today known as Mauritius) in the Indian Ocean. The prize money awarded for this event was considerable, and as with Quilliam, it was probably enough to set Kelly up as a man of property (like Quilliam, Kelly would also become a member of the House of Keys following the close of hostilities). Later he was present at the surrender of Java, and was then posted from *Illustrious* to the command of HMS *Dasher*, an 18-gun sloop. He was entrusted with the dispatches relating to the surrender of Java, and returned with these to Spithead – on the journey he was involved, along with the frigate HMS *Leonidas*, in the capture of a French privateer, *La Confiance*.

Yet Service life in this era was hard. In 1812, Paul Crebbin's brother Lieutenant Thomas Crebbin of the Royal Marines returned to England after some six years and nine months in the tropics, a period of service which greatly damaged his health. He had first embarked on board HMS *Diana* in which ship he was to serve upwards of three years, for part of that time in the West Indies, and during which he was wounded. Afterwards the *Diana* was ordered to the Brazils (modern South America) where he was appointed to HMS *Foudroyant*. She had been in South American waters since March 1808, in the main accompanying convoys. Also in these waters was Captain Peter Heywood, who was serving aboard HMS *Nereus*. In June 1812 he had been ordered to South America in order to safeguard British commerce through Buenos Aires, which was under blockade during the increasingly violent Argentine revolution.

Even after the death of Joseph Clarke however, impressment into the navy continued to be used in the Isle of Man as a punishment for those deemed to be anti-social. A riot in the summer of 1811 had seen a mob attempt to secure the release of a soldier of the 6th Regiment, who had probably been confined in the cells of the Douglas courthouse. One of the officers of the regiment had been assaulted, and a Douglas magistrate had also been verbally threatened, so the Lieutenant Governor Cornelius Smelt had taken drastic steps against the three ringleaders. He informed the Duke of Atholl that:

> I find it my duty to submit to you the propriety of causing directions to be sent to the Regulating Officer of the Impress Service at Liverpool, to send a tender to Castle Town Bay, for those ... who are fit subjects for the sea service, whenever he shall be appraised that they have been found guilty. I am

induced to believe that a measure of this sort might have the effect of putting an end to such disturbances.[99]

Accordingly, early in August 1811, the Royal Navy tender *Maria* arrived at Douglas under the command of a Lieutenant Thomas Hawkes. The lieutenant, on being approached by Norris Moore, the then high-Bailiff, assured the latter that he did not intend to impress any of the fisherman or to interfere with the fishery. Consequently, the men of the Herring fleet continued their occupation till the night of 17 August when several fishermen, working men, and others including soldiers of the Volunteers were impressed after a hard fight, in which some of the men were dangerously wounded. The Duke of Atholl laid the blame for this incident squarely at the door of Smelt, the Lieutenant Governor. He added in a letter to the Westminster government:

> ... the captain of the tender landed and began to impress aided by the soldiers the peaceable inhabitants and scenes of the most disgraceful description ensued; blood was shed and lives lost, the military instead of aiding the civil power joined the press gang and the town of Douglas for several hours bore the appearance ... of a town assaulted and taken by an enemy rather than a town under the protection of law and civil government.[100]

Clearly the soldiers of the 6th Regiment then stationed on the Island had acted in concert with the Navy in rounding up as many men as possible. The situation was volatile, and at low tide a mob estimated at 500 strong tried to reach the tender, shouting 'sink her! Burn her!' So serious did the situation become that Hawkes felt he had no choice but to open fire on them. The *Maria* set off early in the following morning for Ireland. A meeting of the principal inhabitants of Douglas was then held and a memorial presented to the Lieutenant-Governor calling for an investigation of the business. James Drinkwater, who was then mayor of Liverpool, sent a letter to the lords of the Admiralty begging for the release of the impressed fishermen, and received a terse reply, dated 20 August 1811:

> Sir, - In answer to your letter of the 24th instant respecting sundry persons impressed in the Isle of Man by Lieut. Hawes [sic] of the *Maria* tender, I am commanded by my Lords Commissioners of the Admiralty to acquaint you that their Lordships have determined not to discharge these men on account of the very improper conduct of the people of Douglas.[101]

However the Volunteers who were impressed and carried to Dublin were, a few weeks afterwards, liberated by an order from Westminster, and arrived at the Island about the middle of September, to the great joy of their families and friends. On 14 February the following year Douglas had another fright, with the arrival in the port of HMS *Alphea*, which had been damaged in a squall at sea. A 68-foot long schooner built in Bermuda, she carried a crew of thirty-five and ten carronades. She was leaking badly after being caught in the storm, and put into the port for repairs. Two boats from the revenue cutter *Lynx* had to assist her into the harbour, perhaps a sign of her damaged condition, for the ship's log records that her sailmaker spent the next two days repairing her sheets. On Sunday 16 February two landsmen and three boys deserted the ship. Her commander Lieutenant Thomas William Jones gave orders to have them found, or to have the same number impressed, and two parties under petty officers set off to find them. The *Manks Advertiser* records that the Island was in a state of terror and suspense, until on the following Wednesday two of the deserters were brought back by a constable. Thick fog prevented the schooner from sailing until 22 February, when she set off for Ramsey Bay. The log now records:

> At 6 sent the Cutter with a Petty Officer & 4 men on board the merchant ship in the Roads to press[,] at 10 boat returned having impressed one man.[102]

THE NAPOLEONIC WARS

It is not known if the unfortunate pressed man was Manx, but if he was it was unlikely that he saw his home again, for not long afterwards the *Alphea* left Manx waters. About a year later in the English Channel she blew up, during an action with a French ship, and was lost with her entire crew. However, there can be no doubt that for some of the Manx people, sheltering deserters was seen as a way of thumbing their nose at the new regime.

* * *

Whilst Britain was still at war with France, simmering tensions led to a renewed outbreak of hostilities with the United States. The Anglo-American War of 1812 was peripheral to the more significant conflict between Britain and her allies, and the French, though it might be argued that it was caused indirectly by that war. The chief grievance of the United States was British interference in her trade and commerce, through her attempts to control maritime traffic, and the impressment of American sailors into the Royal Navy. To be fair on the British, with the United States as a nation only around thirty years old, it was often quite hard to be certain who was an American and who was not, for many of its citizens were not born in the New World. It was said that one distinctive feature of American sailors was their tendency to wear ear rings, though even this was not foolproof. One crusty British captain, addressing one of his crewmen who sported such jewellery, is reported to have asked if he was a woman or a damned American.

Although there was action on land, and the British famously burned down the White House, the war at sea was arguably more significant as it posed a considerable distraction to the Royal Navy when it was already occupied with the French. Again, there were many Manx seamen who were involved in the conflict. One of the youngest was Baldwin Wake Walker, son of John Walker of Whitehaven and Frances (daughter of Captain Drury Wake, of the 17th Dragoons, and niece of Sir William Wake, eighth baronet). He was born at Port-e-Vullen, near Ramsey in 1802, had entered the Royal Navy in 1812, and was serving as a gentleman volunteer or midshipman at this time.

John Tobin's nephew, John Caesar Tobin, was drowned at Demerara in 1812, aged 18. He had been serving on board the sloop HMS *Bridget*, (Captain Vernon), which on 5 December beat off an American privateer of nineteen guns. On this occasion two men were killed, and the captain, two passengers and four men wounded. During the action, which lasted two hours, young Tobin was reported by the captain to have fought with great spirit. One of the men killed in this battle was also Manx: Alexander McKillar, aged 18, was the grandson of Mr Kerr of Duke Street, Douglas. There were also numerous British vessels holding letters of marque which were involved in this conflict. In 1812 one of these, John Tobin's vessel, the privateer *John Tobin*, had a vigorous fight with an American, in which the latter came off the worst.

Another family with members at sea was that of Senhouse Wilson of Douglas, the Island's Receiver General. In 1812 one of his sons, Daniel F. Wilson was a member of the revenue service on the Island and was the commander of the *Lynx* cutter which patrolled the waters between Liverpool and Douglas, whilst his brother Senhouse was now aboard HMS *Spitfire,* a 14-gun sloop, at Portsmouth. With the outbreak of war the Royal Navy seized all American vessels then in British ports. *Spitfire* was among the Royal Navy vessels then lying at Spithead or Portsmouth, and so entitled to share in the grant for the American ships *Belleville*, *Janus*, *Aeos*, *Ganges* and *Leonidas* seized there on 31 July 1812.

HMS *Spitfire* was in company with *Galatea* when they recaptured the brig *Fermina* on 18 April 1813, and shortly afterwards sailed for American waters. *Spitfire* was cruising with the 32-gun frigate *Alexandria* off North Cape on 19 July 1813. There they chased the 44-gun American frigate *President* and her consort, the privateer schooner *Scourge*, away from a British convoy out of Archangel. Captain John Rodgers of *President* later excused his fleeing from the British by claiming that he had fled from a ship of the line and a frigate. It was whilst he was also serving with the *Spitfire* some years later that a melancholy duty fell to Major Paul

THE NAPOLEONIC WARS

Crebbin, of the Royal Marines; he had to send word to Senhouse Wilson senior in Douglas that his son had died of an illness at the Royal Naval Hospital at Haslar, near Portsmouth.

On 1 June 1813, off Boston Harbor, the United States Navy frigate *Chesapeake*, commanded by Captain James Lawrence, encountered her British counterpart HMS *Shannon* under Captain Philip Broke. The two frigates were of near-identical size. *Chesapeake*'s crew was larger, but most had not served or trained together. The *Shannon* had been loitering close to the mouth of Boston Harbour for several days, and the challenge which she presented was too much for Lawrence to overlook. As she headed out, Broke noted in his log that on the foremast of the *Chesapeake* she carried a white flag proclaiming 'Free Trade and Seamen's Rights', two of the principal reasons for the US declaration of war.

So convinced were the citizens of Boston of another American victory over a British foe that a good number followed her, in private craft, in order to obtain a better view of the spectacle. When the two ships were well out to sea, Broke ordered his ship to slow in order to allow the *Chesapeake* to catch up. The British ship prepared for combat in the usual way – extraneous items were cleared away, grog was served to the men, and livestock was thrown overboard to prevent it getting lose and obstructing the gun crews in the thick of battle. Broke exhorted his men to give their best, after the recent British defeats. As he did so, the *Chesapeake* was closing fast and it appeared for a moment that she might use her extra momentum to sweep past the vulnerable stern of the British frigate, and rake her with a broadside as she did so; but instead, the American reduced his speed and came up alongside the *Shannon* about 40 yards off. Why he gave up his advantage remains unclear, but perhaps he was overly confident given recent American victories. The two vessels traded fire for several minutes with deadly results to both parties; however it soon became clear that the *Chesapeake* was coming off worst as the *Shannon's* carronades swept the enemy deck with flying metal.

In this action, Philip Cosnahan (another son of Deemster John Cosnahan and Catherine Finch, and brother to Michael Cosnahan), was a midshipman on board HMS *Shannon*. Together with Midshipman William Smith, he led the sailors and marines in the tops in killing every American sailor on the enemy decks or in her rigging. Cosnahan in particular climbed out on to a spar to get a better aim, and fired shot after shot as sailors and marines handed him loaded muskets. Not surprisingly he was later specially mentioned in Captain Broke's report of the battle:

> It is impossible to particularize every brilliant deed performed by my officers and men . . . but I must mention, when the ships' yards were locked together that Mr. Cosnahan who commanded in our maintop, finding himself screened from the enemy by the foot of the topsail, laid out on the mainyard to fire upon them and shot three men.[103]

There are several interesting aspects to this heroic act by Cosnahan – it is recorded elsewhere that it was the men in the maintop of the *Shannon* who loaded the muskets, and handed them down to Cosnahan through the 'Lubber's Hole'. The fore and maintops of the *Shannon* were protected by a top cloth which went round outside the rigging and along the toprail, and then across by the heel of the topmast. It concealed the small arms men in the top from the sight of the enemy, but also meant that the muskets could only be handed down to Cosnahan through this small hatch. He killed most of the men in the *Chesapeake*'s mizzentop by this method, but the fact that he could see into the mizzentop at all tells us that by this point in the action, the *Chesapeake*'s taffrail was well before the *Shannon*'s gangway port. By now almost every officer on the American ship was dead or severely injured. Her wheel spun, unattended, as each officer who had tried to take control had been shot in turn, and now the badly damaged *Chesapeake* was drifting out of control. Lawrence was mortally wounded and as he was carried below famously cried out, 'Don't give up the ship! Hold on, men!' However the *Chesapeake* had drifted into contact with the *Shannon* and the two became entangled, as Cosnahan's exploit confirms, and the moment had now come to board her. In spite of the devastating casualties the remaining American crew put up a stiff resistance, but the *Chesapeake* was captured nonetheless.

British citizens reacted with celebration and relief that the run of American victories had ended. Notably, this action was by ratio one of the bloodiest contests recorded during the age of sail, with more dead and wounded than HMS *Victory* suffered in four hours of combat at Trafalgar. Captain Lawrence was killed and Captain Broke was so badly wounded that he never again held a sea command. In spite of his bravery Cosnahan did not reach a higher grade than that of lieutenant; he was drowned less than a year later in January 1813 when the Manx sailing vessel *Union* was lost, (not the *Lord Hill* as is sometimes erroneously recorded) with the whole of the passengers and crew. The *Union* sank by running aground on the Horse Bank, in the middle of the River Ribble. It is said that Cosnahan owed his death to his great agility, for the vessel was actually some yards away from the Red Pier in Douglas, having begun the voyage, when he leaped on board. Be that as it may, it was a bitter irony that the sea should have claimed in this way a man who had faced the danger of battle and survived, and who was now returning to the fray. There was a great outpouring of grief in Douglas at the loss of this young hero, and someone (probably his sister) composed a verse in his memory:

> When God in awful majesty, surveys
> The vast expanse of earth, and air, and seas,
> He deigns to all his care – yet He reserves
> An uncontroul'd command, with which he serves
> The will and wishes of frail souls on earth.
> And, in His power, can change distress to mirth.
> Why then not – must not we – to His command,
> Bow with regard – before whom all must stand?
> The sea– as must the Earth – are at His great call,
> Will freely yield to Him – her choicest all.
> Why then despair, when shortly we shall meet
> With our dear Philip, whom we all regret?

> He's called from toil – and dangers – wars– and fame
> On earth t'enjoy a much more heavenly name,
> Of a true warrior– who serv'd God and man
> And whose renown will endless ages stand.
> He gained with Broke, the Hero of the *Shannon*,
> A name immortal – whilst there's name to cannon:
> And though he's now remov'd – lost in the Union
> Time ne'er will – can't forget – poor Philip Cosnahan.
> He'd lived the life, which leads on high to Sion;
> In him were both combined – the lamb and lion.[104]

Yet there was also considerable anger that this tragic loss was both predictable and avoidable, and one correspondent wrote to a local newspaper to blame the disaster upon a common Manx vice, that of drunkenness among the captain and crew. Cosnahan's grieving father wrote shortly afterwards from Douglas to Lord Melville at the Admiralty:

> I feel it a painful duty to acquaint your Lordship that my son, Philip Cosnahan, late of the *Shannon*, whom your Lordship so graciously recommended for promotion to Admiral Sir J.B. Warren, is no more. Anxious, my lord, to accompany the expedition under Admiral Cochrane, he took his departure from this island for Liverpool, sooner than I wished, in a small vessel, which was lost on the Banks, and every soul perished.
>
> My lord, I cannot but repeat my thanks to your lordship for giving a commission to my son Hugh, late of the *Atlante*, who, poor fellow, from great weakness in consequence of the yellow fever, after near ten years' absence, returned to us, and, thank God, is getting fast well.
>
> I am also, my lord, to return you my heartfelt thanks for the (well earned) commission which I understand your lordship has been graciously pleased to forward to my son, Michael

Finch Cosnahan, now with Sir Home Popham in India. He my lord has been near nine years in almost every species of service, and never once at home. I am proud, my lord, to think that the service cannot boast finer young men that my surviving sons.[105]

Cosnahan's letter brings into focus once more the stories of the other two members of this seafaring trio of brothers. Hugh Cosnahan was commissioned as lieutenant in 1813, after a period of service in the West Indies, whilst Michael had served variously as Midshipman and Master's Mate. He too would pass his lieutenant's examination in the near future, and ended his naval career as a Commander.

✳ ✳ ✳

Returning to the Anglo-American War, in September 1813, Captain John Quilliam, now in command of HMS *Crescent*, took part in the capture of an American privateer, the schooner *Elbridge Gerry*, off Cape Row, Newfoundland, with a crew of sixty-six men. Quilliam had been charged with protecting fishermen using the Newfoundland station. The greatest threat on the eastern seaboard of the USA, particularly to British merchant ships, were American schooners fitted out as privateers. These ships though fast were lightly armed, and would usually come off worst against a British frigate. On this occasion, when the *Elbridge Gerry* sighted the *Crescent* unusually there was almost no breeze. As Quilliam observed them and brought his ship about, he noted in his log that the crew had their oars out and were rowing, so eager were they to outpace the *Crescent*. Quilliam however handled his ship expertly and overhauled the American. Outgunned, she surrendered without a fight. The first man on board was Midshipman named Tobin, a Manxman. The Royal Navy took a dim view of privateer crews. In most cases they refused to exchange them as they did regular naval prisoners, and most of the crew of the *Elbridge Gerry* would be incarcerated in Dartmoor prison.

MANXMEN AT SEA IN THE AGE OF NELSON, 1760–1815

The war in America was still in progress when in April 1814 Napoleon Bonaparte abdicated, his forces having been pushed back from Russia to the gates of Paris. There were celebrations throughout the British Isles as nearly twelve years of war in Europe drew to a close. Even before peace was declared, the Royal Navy was scaling back its operations, and Commander William Kelly wrote rather plaintively to the secretary at the Admiralty seeking another posting:

> I request you will be pleased to lay before the Lords Commissioners of the Admiralty my desire for employment in any way their Lordships may think proper.[106]

The Admiralty now had more officers than it needed, and when Kelly asked for a leave of absence to collect his personal possessions he was told to report to his next posting immediately or not at all. By 1815 he had been given command of HMS *Insolent*, a small sloop based at Plymouth used for recruiting purposes. It was something of a step down from some of the other ships which he had served aboard, but at least he was employed. With the coming of peace however, this was to be his last posting, and he returned to the Isle of Man shortly thereafter.

Epilogue

The Napoleonic and Revolutionary wars cast a long shadow across the years which followed. Many were the ex-sailors among the paupers of the 1820s and 1830s. Growing industrialisation, particularly in agriculture, removed much of the unskilled work which had once been available in winter, further adding to the hardships of the poor. Those who had been wounded or maimed were often in the worst position, abandoned by the government which they had fought to uphold, and reliant upon charity. The many disabled ex-soldiers and ex-sailors in the Isle of Man in the 1820s and 1830s formed a good portion of those for whom church collections and other charitable donations were made. Even those who had some form of pension found it difficult. Henry Waterson of Rushen, an outpatient of Greenwich Hospital, wrote to the commissioners of that institution, informing them that:

> I commenced [my] service in the Royal Navy as sailmaker on board his majesty's *Expedition* cutter commanded by Lieutenant Patrick in the year 1793 & was drafted to the *Irresistable* [sic] commanded by Richard Grindal & had the honour to serve as a quarter master in the Action off Ushant on the 23 of June under Admiral Lord Bridport where [I] received a slight wound. [I] had likewise of service in the said ship commanded by G. Marten in the action off Cape St Vincent on the 14 February 1797 commanded by Admiral Lord St Vincent. [I] was drafted from the *Irresistable* in the year 1798 to the *Ajax* commanded by Alexander Cochran

& served in Egypt where [I] received an impediment in [my] sight which has terminated in total blindness & from which ship was discharged as Quarter master at the peace of 1802 with instructions that if [my] sight should not be restored I should apply to the honourable board for support ... Shortly after [I] was so discharged [I] became totally blind & did petition as directed & was admitted an out pentioner [sic] of the Royal Hospital at greenwich with a pension of £7 per annum. [I] humbly state that £7 per annum is not sufficient to support any Person with the most common necessities of Life & leaves to [me] no alternative between begging & starving in an island where no provision is made for the poor.[107]

Others who had been at sea sometimes fared better. John Cowle who had been aboard the *Temeraire* at Trafalgar and had lost his arm in the battle became a school teacher in the 1820s, and was greatly respected. Hugh Garrett, who had reached the position of Master in the Royal Navy, became a staunch supporter of the Temperance movement in his later years and was remembered as an eloquent public speaker. He was described in his obituary as, 'a faithful and zealous local preacher in the Wesleyan Methodist Connexion'. Thomas Freer, who had reached the rank of Lieutenant in the Royal Navy before the close of hostilities, went on to work for the P and O Line, and successfully made the transition to steam propulsion. He was the captain of the SS *Oriental* at the time of his death.

Captain John Quilliam's reputation was undoubtedly the greatest in the Island after the Napoleonic Wars. He was widely respected, and as a member of the House of Keys was consulted upon many issues. He died relatively young, in 1828, and it was said that notification of his promotion to Admiral arrived on the day he died. By his family in later years he was known as 'Admiral Quilliam', even if the promotion was not officially gazetted.

EPILOGUE

Baldwin Wake-Walker, who began his career during the latter part of this era, did reach that rank in his lifetime. Hugh Crow had been offered a seat in the Keys, but declined. He died in 1829, but left a considerable estate, and money with which he instructed his executors to publish his memoirs. This they did, but they were clearly embarrassed by some of his views on the Africa Trade which were already frowned upon by 1830. Nonetheless, Crow's memoir forms one of the most important documents concerning both slavery and warfare at sea in this era. In his description of him in his 1899 history of the Isle of Man, Edward Callow preferred to concentrate on Crow's exploits against the French, rather than the fact that he enriched himself through slavery, writing:

> Captain Crow was a man that not only every Manxman but every Britisher ... should be justly proud of. Thank goodness there are many more like him both afloat and on shore![108]

As far as the Isle of Man was concerned, as an inexpensive place to live it quickly acquired a reputation among retired officers of the army and navy, who came to the Island in droves. Here they could make their half-pay stretch much further, and could live the life of modest gentlemen, something often unaffordable in England. A number of Nelson's captains are buried in the churchyards of the Island as a result of this trend.

Economically things slowly began to improve, as tourism which had begun during the wars in a small way gradually became a mass phenomenon, and the Island built its reputation as a holiday mecca for the middle and working classes of northern England as the nineteenth century progressed. During this time, the Isle of Man almost completely re-invented itself as a pleasure paradise, the home of happy holidays, and in the process its rather darker image as a 'nest of smugglers' and as a place where some of the hardiest and best seafarers in the world were to be found was almost entirely forgotten. Douglas Fort was pulled down, and its remnant subsumed into the Victoria Pier. St Matthew's church on the harbourside was demolished with little sentimentality in 1899, although St George's church still stands. The old parts of Douglas which were so closely associated with Bligh and Christian were swept away in the 'improvements' of the 1930s and even the Nunnery where Peter Heywood was born was re-built in neo-Gothic style in the Victorian era. Only Peter John Heywood's house (later the Douglas Hotel) still stands though having suffered many humiliations over recent years and narrowly avoiding demolition. Yet it survives as a reminder of this turbulent era.

Notes

Chapter 1

1. Manx National Heritage Episcopal, Wills, Ballaugh 1753, Daniel Cottiman
2. John Newton, *Thoughts on the African Slave Trade*, London 1788, p.8
3. Manx National Heritage, MS 09707, Atholl Papers X-35 013
4. Isle of Man Natural History and Antiquarian Society, *Proceedings* Vol 4 #4, 1939
5. Manx National Heritage Episcopal Wills, Maughold 1759-2, Ewan Garret
6. Manx National Heritage Episcopal Wills, Marown 1764, Thomas Cubbon
7. Manx National Heritage Episcopal Wills, German 1762, William Lace
8. Manx National Heritage Episcopal Wills, Maughold 1765, William Kneen
9. *The Universal Magazine of Knowledge and Pleasure*, John Hinton, London, March 1760, p.161
10. *Manx Sun*, 26 November 1904
11. Charles Roeder, *Manx Notes & Queries*, Douglas, 1904
12. Gomer Williams, *Liverpool Privateers*, London 1897, p.486
13. The National Archives, ADM 106/1201/269
14. The National Archives, ADM 106/1185/171
15. The National Archives, ADM 106/1168/81
16. Rupert Furneaux, *Tobias Furneaux Circumnavigator*, London, 1960, p.145
17. Manx National Heritage, MS00669a

Chapter 2

18. Isle of Man Natural History and Antiquarian Society, *Proceedings* Vol 4 #3, 1939
19. Manx National Heritage Episcopal, Wills, Marown, 1784-1, Thomas Gell
20. *Ramsey Church Magazine*, 1897-1898
21. A.W. Moore, *Manx Worthies*, Douglas 1901, p.173
22. *Ramsey Church Magazine*, July 1898
23. *The Scots Magazine* Vol 42, Sands, Brymer, Murray and Cochran, 1780, p.545
24. Hugh Crow, *The Memoirs of Captain Hugh Crow*, Oxford, 2007, p.16
25. William Harrison, *Manx Miscellanies*, Edinburgh, 1880, p.7
26. Manx National Heritage, MS09591, Robert Parry Young
27. Manx National Heritage, MS 02679c, George Moore II
28. Mitchell Library, State Library of New South Wales, MLMSS 1016
29. *Journal of the Manx Museum* Vol III No 471936, p.110
30. James Scurry, *The Captivity, Sufferings and Escape of James Scurry*, p.27
31. Ibid, p.46
32. Manx National Heritage Episcopal Wills GL721, 1782, Book 1 Will 272
33. *Journal of the Manx Museum* Vol IV No 59, 1939, p.130
34. The National Archives, ADM 51/356
35. Crow, *Memoirs*, p.17
36. Manx National Heritage Episcopal Wills, Braddan 1784, Ewan Karran
37. Manx National Heritage, MS00669a
38. William Bligh correspondence, Mitchell Library, State Library of New South Wales – Safe 1/40
39. Manx National Heritage, MS 09381/8/5 (1)
40. Edward Christian, *A Short Reply to Captain William Bligh's Answer*, London, 1795
41. Owen Rutter, *Turbulent Journey A Life of William Bligh*, London, 1936, p.75

NOTES

42. Manx National Heritage, P.1817, Fannin map
43. David Robertson, *A Tour through the Isle of Man*, London, 1794, p.7

Chapter 3

44. Manx National Heritage, Taubman Papers, MS09591
45. Bligh correspondence, Mitchell Library, State Library of New South Wales, Safe 1/45
46. Manx National Heritage, MS 09381/8/5 (1)
47. John Marshall, *Royal Naval Biography* Vol II Part II, London, 1825, p.774
48. Ibid, p.776
49. Manx National Heritage, MS 09381/8/5 (1)
50. Mitchell Library, State Library of New South Wales, Safe 1/45
51. Manx National Heritage, MS 09381/8/5 (1)
52. Ibid
53. Manx National Heritage, MS 09519
54. Crow, *Memoirs*, p.197
55. Ibid, p.32
56. *The Naval Chronicle*, Vol 25, London, 1811, p.7
57. *Dublin Chronicle*, 14 July 1791

Chapter 4

58. Crow, *Memoirs*, p.45
59. *Manks Mercury*, 2 April 1793
60. *Manks Mercury*, 30 April 1793
61. *The Mariner's Mirror* Vol 64 No 4, London, 1978, p.361
62. Crow, *Memoirs*, p.56
63. Manx National Heritage, MS 09707, Atholl Papers X/36-7
64. Crebbin Papers, courtesy of the Walker family

65. *The Scots Magazine* Vol 57, Edinburgh, January 1795, p.465
66. William Richard O'Byrne, *A Naval Biographical Dictionary*, London, 1849, p.1338
67. Manx National Heritage, MS 00920/1
68. Manx National Heritage, MS 00920/2 C
69. Williams, *Liverpool Privateers*, p.349
70. John Feltham, *A Tour Through the Isle of Man*, Douglas, 1861, p.78
71. The National Archives, ADM 1/1624
72. Ibid
73. Ibid
74. Memoirs and proceedings – Manchester Literary Society Vol 45, 1900-1901, p.37
75. Manx National Heritage, MS 06365/1, Callister Notebook
76. Crebbin Papers, courtesy of the Walker family
77. Crow, *Memoirs*, p.57
78. T. Sturges Jackson, *Logs of the Great Sea Fights*, Vol II, London, 1900, p.119
79. Liverpool Record Office 387 MD42, Account book of ship *Lottery*

Chapter 5

80. The National Archives, ADM 354/213/32
81. The National Archives, ADM 354/214/314
82. Edward Fraser, *Champions of the Fleet*, London, 1908, p.230
83. Isle of Man Public Record Office, A58 Liber Plitor
84. *Manx Sun*, 9 December 1905
85. *Manks Advertiser*, 12 September 1807
86. Edward Fraser, *The Sailors whom Nelson led*, London, 1913, p.269
87. The National Archives, ADM 51/4514
88. A.W. Moore, *The Letters of Lieutenant Edward Christian*, Douglas, 1898
89. *Liverpool Chronicle*, 19 February 1806

NOTES

90. Crebbin Papers, courtesy of the Walker family
91. *Manx Advertiser*, 16 August 1806
92. William James, *Naval History of Great Britain* Vol IV, London, 1826, p.434
93. Moore, *The Letters of Lieutenant Edward Christian*
94. Manx National Heritage, MS00669a
95. *Manks Advertiser*, 2 November 1811
96. National Archives of Canada, Ottawa, Admiralty 1: Secretary's Department: In-letters, Adm. 1/498
97. National Archives of Canada, Ottawa, C.O. 217/83
98. The National Archives, ADM 1/2373
99. Manx National Heritage, Atholl Papers X29-3/4
100. Manx National Heritage, Atholl Papers X29-21
101. *Peel City Guardian*, 21 September 1901
102. The National Archives, ADM 51/2099
103. *The Gentleman's Magazine*, Vol 83, Part 2, p.280
104. *Isle of Man Weekly Gazette*, 10 February 1814
105. J.G. Brighton, *Admiral Sir P.B.V. Broke, Bart, A Memoir*, London, 1866, p.452
106. The National Archives, ADM/1/2026

Epilogue

107. Manx National Heritage, MS00669a
108. Edward Callow, *From King Orry to Queen Victoria*, London, 1899, p.169

Bibliography

Brighton, J.G., *Admiral Sir P.B.V. Broke, Bart, A Memoir*, London, 1866
Callow, Edward, *From King Orry to Queen Victoria*, London, 1899
Christian, Edward, *A Short Reply to Captain William Bligh's Answer*, London, 1795
Crow, Hugh, *The Memoirs of Captain Hugh Crow*, Oxford, 2007
Feltham, John, *A Tour through the Isle of Man*, Douglas, 1861
Fraser, Edward, *Champions of the Fleet*, London, 1908
Fraser, Edward, *The Sailors whom Nelson led*, London, 1913
Furneaux, Rupert, *Tobias Furneaux Circumnavigator*, London, 1960
Harrison, William, *Manx Miscellanies*, Edinburgh, 1880
James, William, *Naval History of Great Britain*, London, 1826
Moore, A.W., *The Letters of Lieutenant Edward Christian*, Douglas, 1898
Moore, A.W., *Manx Worthies*, Douglas, 1901
Newton, John, *Thoughts on the African Slave Trade*, London, 1788
O'Byrne, William Richard, *A Naval Biographical Dictionary*, London, 1849
Robertson, David, *A Tour through the Isle of Man*, London, 1794
Roeder, Charles, *Manx Notes & Queries*, Douglas, 1904
Rutter, Owen, *Turbulent Journey A Life of William Bligh*, London, 1936
Scurry, James, *The captivity, sufferings and escape of James Scurry who was detained a prisoner during ten years in the dominions of Hyder Ali and Tippoo Saib, Written by himself*, London, H. Fisher 1824
Sturges-Jackson, T., *Logs of the Great Sea Fights*, London, 1900

BIBLIOGRAPHY

Taggart, Edward, *A memoir of the late Captain Peter Heywood, R. N.; with extracts from his diaries and correspondence*, London, 1832

Townley, Richard, *A Journal Kept in the Isle of Man*, Whitehaven, 1791

Williams, Gomer, *History of the Liverpool privateers and letters of marque with an account of the Liverpool slave trade*, Heinemann, London, 1897

Index

1812, War of, 143–7, 149

American War of Independence, 27–61, 75, 79, 84, 138
Atholl, 2nd Duke of (John Murray), 1, 15, 17
Atholl, 3rd Duke of (James Murray), 17–18
Atholl, 4th Duke of (John Murray), 26, 63–4, 75, 80, 115, 140–1
Australia, 27, 44, 61, 73, 76

Bacon, John Joseph, 39–41, 43, 114
Bacon, John Errington, 43
Bacon, Captain Joseph, 89–90
Bechinoe, Lieutenant Benjamin, 25
Bligh, Elizabeth, 45–6, 56, 63, 69
Bligh, Lieutenant William, 21, 25, 42, 44–6, 55–6, 58, 61–6, 68–71, 78, 154
Borwick, Lieutenant Halley, 19–20
Brew, Stephen, 29
Bridson, John, 4
Bridson, Thomas, 4
Bristol, 43

Cable, Captain Samuel, 80, 83, 98–101, 103, 113–14
Calf of Man, 19
Callister, Thomas, 103–105
Camperdown, Battle of, 98
Cape of Good Hope, 44, 65, 93
Cape Horn, 22, 65
Cape St Vincent, Battle of, 97
Carlisle, 11
Carroll, Thomas, 54–5
Chesapeake, Battle of the, 49–50
Christian, Charles, 64–5, 69, 71
Christian, Evan, 132
Christian, Acting Lieutenant Fletcher, 56–7, 61–73, 78, 154
Christian, Humphrey, 56, 63, 73–4
Clarke, Captain Edward, 113, 124
Clarke, Lieutenant Joseph, 113–18, 124, 140
Colby, Robert, 49–50
Cook, Captain James, 21–2, 25, 44, 61–2, 66
Copenhagen, Battle of, 109, 130
Cork, 16, 38–9
Cosnahan, Hugh, 33, 35
Cosnahan, Lieutenant Hugh, 129

INDEX

Cosnahan, Captain James, 82
Cosnahan, John, 35, 129, 145
Cosnahan, Michael Finch, 129, 145
Cosnahan, Midshipman Philip, 145–8
Cottier, Robert, 50–2
Cottiman, William, 3
Cowl, John, 46–7
Crebbin, Lieutenant Paul, 91, 106, 140, 145
Crebbin, Philip, 126
Crebbin, Thomas (uncle), 10–11
Crebbin, Thomas (nephew), 90–1, 140
Cregan, Patrick, 2
Crellin, Thomas, 134–5
Cretney, Thomas, 44
Crigan, Alexander, 133
Crow, Captain Hugh, 38, 54, 73–4, 80, 87–8, 96, 107–108, 125, 133, 153
Crow, William, 30
Cubbon, Thomas, 9–10
Curphy, William, 7, 8
Curwen, John Christian, 63, 71

Dessau, Francis John, 53
Dogger Bank, Battle of, 45
Douglas, 2–3, 6, 9, 15, 17, 19, 21, 24–6, 29–30, 32–5, 37, 39–40, 44–6, 53, 56, 59–64, 66, 70, 73, 75–6, 80–3, 85, 89–90, 92, 97, 99, 101, 106, 115–18, 127–9, 134–5, 140–2, 144–5, 147–8, 153–4
Dowe, George, 2
Dublin, 13, 19, 36–7, 142

Elliott, Captain John, 13–15

Fannin, Peter, 18, 21–6, 39, 45, 59
Fargher, Thomas, 87
Fishermen, 1, 60, 99–101, 103, 113, 115, 118, 141–2, 149
Fleming, Lieutenant John, 83
Franklin, President Benjamin, 31
Frissell, Lieutenant William, 87, 136, 137
Furneaux, Captain Tobias, 22, 45

Gale, Thomas, 29–30
Garret, Ewan, 8
Gell, John, 38–41
Geneste, Lewis, 33–4
Gibraltar, 36, 104, 123
Groix, Battle of, 89–90

Halifax (Nova Scotia), 12, 107, 135
Herring Fleet, 56, 59–60, 98, 99, 100–102, 113, 118, 141
Heywood, 'Nessy', 15, 73
Heywood, Captain Peter, 15, 63–6, 68–70, 72–3, 78, 85–7, 140, 154
Heywood, Peter John, 15, 26, 35, 63–4, 154

MANXMEN AT SEA IN THE AGE OF NELSON, 1760–1815

Hillyar, Admiral James, 21
Hyder Ali, 48–9

Impressment, 6–7, 9–11, 29, 34, 38, 40–2, 44, 46, 52–4, 74, 77, 80, 83, 89, 99, 100–103, 113, 115–18, 122, 125, 136–7, 140–3
Inman, Lieutenant Henry, 74–5, 80

Johnstone, Captain George, 37, 44
Jones, Captain John Paul, 32–3

Kelly, Captain William, 53, 55, 93, 139, 150
Keppel, Commodore Augustus, 7
Kermeen, Anthony, 55
Kingston (Jamaica), 34, 108, 124
Kneale, Captain Charles, 111
Kneen, William, 11–12

Lace, William, 10
Lawson, John, 122
Lewin, John, 9
Lewin, Paul, 47, 49
Liverpool, 3–4, 15–16, 33, 40–2, 53, 57, 74, 76, 80–2, 87–8, 95–6, 99, 107, 111, 116, 124–5, 127, 132, 140–1, 144, 148
Locker, Captain William, 51
Lockhart, Lieutenant William, 20
London, 14, 27–8, 30–1, 54, 57, 62, 64, 105, 109, 127
Louisbourg, 8–9

McNally, Richard, 29
Manx language, 12, 18, 30, 40, 88, 122
Marines, 15, 23, 43, 65, 89–92, 106, 121, 129–30, 140, 145–6
Moore, Sir George, 6
Moore, George, 43
Moore, Rev Philip, 14, 26, 32, 35
Moore, Captain Thomas, 36–7
Moore, William, 53

Nelson, Admiral Lord, 21, 51, 105, 108, 118–23, 127
New York, 11, 30, 31
New Zealand, 22–4
Newton, John, 4–5

Onchan, 25, 30, 45, 78, 134

Pasley, Admiral Thomas, 15, 19, 44, 46, 63, 73, 87
Point of Ayre, Battle of, 13
Portsmouth, 7, 21, 29, 39, 45, 77, 89, 93, 144–5
Press Gang *see* Impressment
Prisoners of War, 15, 37, 39–40, 47–8, 87–8, 90, 104, 122, 133–4, 149
Prize Money, 7, 43, 50, 105–106, 127, 139
Privateers, 6, 12, 16, 29, 32–6, 39, 43, 46, 81–3, 87, 89, 95, 97, 107, 111, 123–5, 138, 140, 144, 149

INDEX

Qualtrough, Captain Richard, 34–5, 37
Quayle, Midshipman Edward, 94, 105
Quilliam, Captain John, 77–8, 93, 98, 105–106, 109–10, 119–21, 123, 127, 131, 133, 138–9, 149, 152

Ramsey, 11, 13–15, 34, 38, 54, 87, 97, 114, 134–5, 142–3
Revestment, Act of, 18–19, 28, 32, 45
Royal Navy, 6, 9–10, 12–13, 16, 18–19, 21, 24–6, 28–31, 34, 37–8, 41, 46, 49, 52–3, 55, 60, 62–3, 69, 72, 74–6, 78, 80, 83–5, 87, 89, 92–3, 98, 101, 105–106, 108, 112, 116–18, 122, 125–7, 129–32, 136, 138–9, 141, 143–4, 149–52

Seven Years War, 1–28, 90, 112
Shimin, Captain Radcliffe, 95–6
Ships:
  Achille, 122
  Adamant, 83
  Adventure, 22, 24
  Aeolus, 13, 15
  Africa, 121
  Ajax, 128–9, 151
  Albemarle, 76
  Alexandria, 138–9, 144

Alfred, 54
Alphea, 142–3
Amazon, 109–10
Ann, 80
Ann (privateer), 82
Ann & Susanna, 81
Anne, 89
Arrogant, 93
Asia, 106
Bahama, 122
Basilisk, 18
Belle Poule, 45
Bellerophon, 86–7
Belleisle (French), 13–14
Belleisle (HMS), 119, 138
Bethia, 62
Blanche, 80, 109
Bonne Citoyenne, 97
Bounty, 61–3, 65–6, 68–72, 76, 78
Brilliant, 13
Brunswick, 131
Bucentaure, 120
Calcutta, 135
Cambridge, 104
Captain, 104–105
Carcass, 19
Centurion, 122
Chesapeake, 137, 145–7
Cholmondley, 19
Christian, 90
Crescent, 139, 149
Dankbaarheid, 44

Dart, 125
De Jonge Jessie Wittween de Lemmer, 35
Deal Castle, 11
Diana, 140
Dolphin, 31
Douglas, 15
Dublin, 9
Dudgeon, 82
Duke, 80
Duke of Argyle, 4
Duke of Atholl, 127
Echo, 53, 93
Elbridge Gerry, 149
Elizabeth, 74
Enterprise, HMS, 10
Enterprise (privateer), 43
Entreprenante, 122
Esther, 19–20, 25, 29
Ethalion, 105–106
Euruyalus, 121
Eurydice, 57
Fame, 36–7
Ferret, 19–21, 25
Fly, 82
Fox, 51–2
Gipsy, 81
Garland, 19
Gorgon, 73
Gregson, 87
Hannibal, 47
Hibernia, 90
Illustrious, 139

Indomptable, 86
Insolent, 150
Intrepid, 49
Invincible, 86
Irresistible, 151
James, 81
Jane, 81
John, 81
John Tobin, 144
Juno, 87
Jupiter, 44, 46
King George, 97
Kitty's Amelia, 125
L'Univers, 36
La Blonde, 13
la Perkin, 82
Le Courrier National, 92
Legere, 105
Les Deux Freres, 36–7
Leviathan, 86, 121
Lexington, 31
Lion, 77, 93, 139
Lord Stanley, 108
Lottery, 111
Lowestoff, 51
Lurcher, 19
Lynx, 142, 144
Marquis of Granby, 15
Marseillois, 36, 49
Maria, 141
Mary, 82, 125
Middlesex, 65, 71
Molly, 81

INDEX

Nancy, 37
Nancy Jenkins, 43
Neptune, 104, 139
Nereus, 140
Nonsuch, 53
Orion, 86
Pallas, 13
Pandora, 72
Perseus, 87
Phaeton, 104
Pigmy, 75
Plumper, 136–7
Pompée, 129
Powerful, 63
President, 144
Prince Edward, 7
Prince George, 93
Prince of Wales, 96
Princess Elizabeth, 82
Princess Royal, 96
Queen, 86
Queen Charlotte, 78, 85–6
Raisonnable, 29–30
Ramillies, 94
Ranger, HMS, 19–21, 24–5, 44
Ranger, USS, 32–3
Redbridge, 126
Redoutable, 120
Rein Deer, 124
Reprisal, 31
Resolution, 21–2, 44
Revenge, 122
Richard, 82

Richmond, 19
Romney, 37
Rose, 12
Royal Sovereign, 120
Russell, 89, 109
*St Alban*s, 106–107
Salamander, 7
Salisbury, 4
Santisima Trinidad, 120
Severn, 42
Shannon, 145–6, 148
Sincerity, 2
Six Sisters, 39
Shrewsbury, 49–50
Spencer, 133
Spider, 101–103
Spitfire, 144
Squirrel, 136
Superb, 46
Tarleton, 96
Temeraire, 120, 152
Terpsichore, 13
Terrible, HMS, 30
Terrible (French), 85
Thetis, HMS, 91
Thetis (treasure ship), 105–106
Thorn, 92
Three Friends, 114
Tickler, 51
Toms, 96
Trelawney, 81
Trente-et-un Mai, 85
Tribune, 90

Triumph, 93, 98
Tyger, 33–5, 37, 44
Tyrannicide, 86
Union, 147–8
Valiant, 86
Van Trompe, 93
Vanguard, 126
Victory, 80, 119–20, 123, 127, 147
Will, 107
William, 83
Wolf, 18
Wolverine, 125
Zephir, 37
Slave Trade, 2–5, 15–16, 32–3, 61–2, 73–4, 80–1, 87–8, 92, 95–6, 107, 111, 123, 125, 138–9, 153
Smuggling, 1, 5, 18, 19, 82, 114, 135, 139
Spain, 6, 16, 28, 31–2, 36, 39, 74–5, 94, 97, 118

Tahiti, 22, 62, 66, 69, 72
Taubman, Major John, 41–2, 58, 63, 69, 71, 90, 103
Thurot, Captain Francois, 12–14
Trafalgar, Battle of, 113, 119–23, 127, 129, 147, 152
Truscott, Captain William, 53

Waldron, George, 2
Walker, Midshipman Baldwin Wake, 143
West Indies, 1, 3, 9, 16, 19, 31, 34, 36, 38, 46, 50, 53–5, 60–2, 95, 105, 123, 126, 136, 138, 140, 149
Whitehaven, 2, 32–3, 35, 38, 57, 143

Young, Robert Benjamin, 24–5, 53, 92, 97, 122–3
Young, Robert Parry, 25, 41–2, 53, 75–7